BRIGHT NOTES

GIANTS IN THE EARTH BY OLE ROLVAAG

Intelligent Education

Nashville, Tennessee

BRIGHT NOTES: Giants in the Earth
www.BrightNotes.com

No part of this publication may be used or reproduced in any manner whatsoever without written permission, except in the case of brief quotations in critical articles and reviews. For permissions, contact Influence Publishers http://www.influencepublishers.com.

ISBN: 978-1-645423-82-9 (Paperback)
ISBN: 978-1-645423-83-6 (eBook)

Published in accordance with the U.S. Copyright Office Orphan Works and Mass Digitization report of the register of copyrights, June 2015.

Originally published by Monarch Press.
Herbert Reaske, 1965
2020 Edition published by Influence Publishers.

Interior design by Lapiz Digital Services. Cover Design by Thinkpen Designs.

Printed in the United States of America.

Library of Congress Cataloging-in-Publication Data forthcoming.
Names: Intelligent Education
Title: BRIGHT NOTES: Giants in the Earth
Subject: STU004000 STUDY AIDS / Book Notes

CONTENTS

1)	Introduction to Ole Rolvaag	1
2)	Detailed Summary of Giants in the Earth: Textual Analysis	10
	Book I—The Land-Taking—Chapters 1-3	10
3)	Giants in the Earth: Textual Analysis	23
	Book I: The Land-Taking - Chapters 4-6	23
	Book II: Founding The Kingdom - Chapters 1-2	37
	Book II: Founding The Kingdom - Chapters 3-4	55
4)	Character Summarization	66
5)	Contemporary Society	78
6)	Concluding Commentary	90
7)	Essay Questions and Answers	108
8)	Bibliography and Guide to Further Research	117

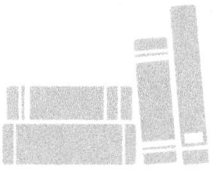

OLE ROLVAAG

INTRODUCTION

THE PERSPECTIVE

South Dakota, nicknamed the Sunshine State, is the state where *Giants in the Earth* takes place. Just as sunshine brings brightness, warmth and happiness, so these qualities pervade this story. Similarly, as sharper shadows come with brighter sun, deep, dark, even frightening episodes intensify this extraordinary novel. The author was born in Norway, where the winters are severe and dreary, but where in summer the sun shines at midnight. A keen awareness of contrast, light and dark, was as deep with Rolvaag as the ocean he crossed when, at the age of twenty, he came to the American prairie.

THE PRAIRIE

The story, whose subtitle is "A Saga of the Prairie," gets its title from the book of Genesis in the Bible. Most people remember the story of Noah's ark and some remember why Jehovah sent the flood, but few recall that a few verses before Noah's account begins, we read: "There were giants in the earth in those days; and also, after that, when the sons of God came in unto the daughters of men, and they bear children to them, the same became mighty men which were of old, men of renown."

When he called his pioneers "giants in the earth," Rolvaag had the whole of this verse in mind. He writes of strong, lusty, confident, joyous men, but behind this vitality the shadow that God may strike again is ever lurking. An understanding of the meaning of the title doesn't alter, however, the subtitle because it is the sense of the prairie, its sunshine, its windswept grass, its fertility, its rich Americanism that lingers well after the book's last page has been turned.

Rolvaag is a down-to-earth writer. He is usually thought of as a realist, but his **realism** is never sordid. His writing is not self-conscious. It is exuberant. Every moment of the "now" is throbbing with the future. The story's leading character, Per Hansa, is an enthusiast. But for all his vigor, Per Hansa is a tragic figure. Rolvaag's **realism** could not have him otherwise. The transition from pioneering to Americanization was rugged physically and also psychologically.

The changes in the prairie that the pioneers bring about are strikingly depicted. Although realistic details are not omitted, Rolvaag never swamps the reader in them. His descriptive passages are never long-winded. Scenes are visualized at a glance. Whereas it is undoubtedly true that the prairie influences the settlers, it never dominates. The people, with their drives, their sense of destiny, win the contest. It is their human qualities that interest. Each character is personal. Each grows in his own way.

THE MANUSCRIPT

When Rolvaag was half way through writing *Giants in the Earth* and was going back to Norway to finish it, he stopped off at Chicago. The harshness of American city life bothered him. He also stopped off in Washington, D.C. He happened to arrive there on the day Woodrow Wilson died. He was shocked by the apathy of the American public. The people in the capital seemed unmoved by the passing of a great man.

Wilson was revered by the foreign-born. Up to the time of his presidency and World War I, the nationalities that were contributing to the American melting pot jealously maintained their various different characteristics and held themselves apart. It was Wilson who brought them together. His distillation gave a country to the men without countries.

Rolvaag was saddened that America was too busy to remember Wilson, too busy to remember the past. On the ship, as he traveled east, he reluctantly decided that one had to be born in Europe to have a sense of the past. At the same time, he knew that Europeans themselves were unconscious of the "Spirit of the Ages" that physically and culturally met them at the turn of nearly every street corner. It was only when Europeans crossed the Atlantic that they felt the absence of a sense of history. History localizes men in time. It gives them a sense of identity.

Rolvaag decried this lack in Americans. He didn't want his beloved Norwegian-Americans, his own children, to forget their past. He thought that in 1924 it was important that they remember the Per Hansas who had settled the prairie. He thought they should also cherish the folkways the pioneers had brought with them. The older generation of Norwegian-Americans believed this strongly. As a member of the newer generation - he became a citizen in 1908 - Rolvaag wanted to sustain them. That is primarily why he became a professor of the Norwegian language and literature in an American university, why he made several trips back to Norway, and why he wrote *Giants in the Earth*.

BIOGRAPHY

Rolvaag, who was forty-seven years old when he began to write *Giants in the Earth*, said he had been preparing for it all his life. He was twenty when he came to this country in 1896. At that time, however, he was no raw lad. He had already served his apprenticeship as a fisherman and had been offered, if he would give up the idea of emigrating, the command of a fine brand-new ship which in a short time he would own. It would be hard to understand why he didn't accept the proposition if one didn't know more about his psychological makeup. In the first place, his father was not just another fisherman descended from a long line of fishermen. The ancestral home where Ole Edvart was born and whence the family took its name was the fishing camp of Rolvaag on the northeast coast. The house was like a big barn, roomy enough for its inhabitants to stretch, make, and repair the fishing nets, twist the ropes, store and prepare the food for a large family, and weave cloth - until he was fifteen, all of the author's clothing was homemade. This same space was also the scene of much reading. His father, a voracious reader, read aloud to his children and supplemented their schooling.

The school, seven and a half miles away, was open but nine weeks a year, with terms of three weeks each. With the exception of the winter term, when the boys boarded at a nearby farm, the fifteen-mile round trip was made daily Ole started school at the age of seven. He, along with his older brother, picked up as they went quite a troop of children. There were as many as sixty-five children in the school. Religious education dominated the curriculum. Almost every day someone was flogged.

Ole wasn't good at school. This disappointed his father because the boy was a great reader at home. It is interesting that Tennyson was an early favorite. When Ole was thirteen, his father's older brother was appointed a permanent teacher in the area's largest town. Ole's father, who had considerable intellectual power of his own, was probably a little jealous of his brother's achievement, but also disappointed that his Ole Edvart was less interested in what took place at school than in the boisterous, rollicking, fighting, sometimes romantic return trips home from school that kept him out till eight at night.

The sooner Ole was graduated, the better. Finally, at fifteen he was confirmed and became a junior member of the fishing fleet. Ole was big. He was a success in the boats. He loved the sea. He enjoyed a storm. Once, when he was alone in a boat, the sea nearly claimed him. He could hardly make it to shore. He was desperate. It took not only his full strength, but more. This over exertion caused a permanent damage to his heart - a heart that was to pain him many times before it dramatically killed him.

For six winters he followed the sea. He was proud, headstrong, and a leader among men. On shore he enjoyed himself immensely. One Christmas season he boasted of going to thirteen dances. He had a series of young loves.

Meantime he continued to read, between other works, large sections of the Bible. He wanted to read more, to travel beyond the Lofoten fishing grounds, to reach the land of Canaan. The promised land beckoned. Yet he didn't want to leave the family he loved. He had a new sweetheart who he hoped might join it. Then came a passage ticket from his uncle in South Dakota. It seemed to him that fate intervened. It was his destiny to go. Something beyond his control drove him. He left. When he arrived at Elk Point, South Dakota, the true pioneering days were already history.

When Rolvaag arrived, he joined three single men who worked a large farm. He immediately began to earn more money than he thought possible. This was his only encouragement because the fisher boy thought farm life almost intolerable.

In a letter dated August 20, 1897, he writes: "It may be that America is a Canaan, but it will be some time before I say so. If my energy is to be drained as it has been hitherto, I won't live long enough to say it at all. Last winter, I weighed 180 pounds. The other day I thought I would see how much I had gained on all the good food I had had. Well, the scale showed barely 140. If I continue at this rate, I won't be a husky man when I get back home."

His idea was to pay back his uncle for his ticket and then save for his return. He was unbearably lonely. There were even fewer books than at home. After a long period he heard about a Scandinavian newspaper, to which he soon subscribed. He began driving to a nearby town. The people were friendly. He learned a little English. He was less lonely. When his uncle left the farm to start one of his own, Ole did not go with him. Instead he decided to go to school. This he knew he never could do in Norway.

SCHOOL IN AMERICA

In 1899, with the encouragement of the local Lutheran minister, he began school at St. Augustana Academy, a preparatory boarding school. On entrance, Rolvaag was twenty-three and sported a fine, thick handlebar mustache. He worked for his room and board, but this did not make him socially unacceptable because many men, though usually younger, were doing the same. Instruction at St. Augustana was in Norwegian. (Although it has since moved to Sioux Falls, South Dakota, this school is still in existence.) Rolvaag surprised himself by graduating with honors. Again encouraged by the ministers, he went in 1901 to St. Olaf's College in Northfield, Minnesota. On his arrival he had forty dollars in his pocket, which was forty dollars more than he had on the day he got off the ship from Norway.

One of his fellow students was John Berdahl, who was to become, years later, his brother-in-law. It was the Berdahl family that supplied much of the pioneer story and history of the area that Rolvaag used later in *Giants in the Earth*. There was a wide difference between the serious settlers of the '70s and their fun-loving descendants in the college. Popular as he was on the campus, Rolvaag's own serious side frequently and privately condemned the students as dull and unthinking human beings. He believed there was pioneering work to be done to save them from the evils of prosperity. In school he criticized not only the students but also their indulgent farmer parents to whom he tried to sell books during the summer vacations. The mellowness of the old Norwegian culture, he felt, was disappearing from their daily lives. It seemed that the art of living was less understood by them than by those who first arrived on the prairie and huddled with their animals in leaky sod houses.

Even in his early student days Rolvaag was disturbed by materialism. The pioneers, he was convinced, had paid a great spiritual price for their material successes. He also was beginning to realize that it was his destiny to strive for a revival of Old World culture. The pioneering spirit and "Spirit of the Ages" must survive and go hand in hand. These are two forces in life that he symbolizes in *Giants in the Earth*. The essence of the book is the relationship between Per Hansa, the strong, confident, physically courageous pioneer, and Beret, his refined, sensitive, and loving wife. First one is in the ascendancy, then the other. *Giants in the Earth* is at once a bold adventure story and a deeply moving study of personal tragedy.

LITERARY COMPETITION

Giants in the Earth was not the first pioneer story of the prairie. The turn of the century had produced many which pleased the reading public when the popularity of Civil War stories declined. Willa Cather's *My Antonia* carried this kind of book to a new literary high point. It was immediately acclaimed for its superior craftsmanship in 1918. Did Rolvaag have any idea that his own pioneer story would be compared with hers? There is no evidence that he ever entertained such an idea. Rolvaag undertook his writing early in 1942 because of an event far removed from the American literary scene. The popular Norwegian novelist, Johan Bojer, announced that he intended to write a novel, in Norwegian, of course, which he intended to call *The Emigrant*. This story was to be written from the viewpoint of the Norwegian who stayed at home, but was nevertheless to be a rendering of the life of the settlers in America. Rolvaag, who had been preparing such a book for many years, was afraid that his book would appear too late for him to avoid an accusation of plagiarism. The knowledge that he must write his book in Norwegian compounded his fears. By this time he spoke English well, but he said Joseph Conrad (a famous English novelist whose first language was Polish) was the exception to prove the rule that man writes best in his native tongue. Bojer, who had enjoyed previous literary successes, was formidable competition. Had Rolvaag not been so convinced that he had a more gripping story to tell and that it was his destiny to write it, he would never have had the courage to begin.

Note on the Pronunciation Of Norwegian Names

O is pronounced as the u in but.
A or AA as the o in order.
OI, OJ, as the oy in coy.
EI or EJ as the a in at e.
BJ as the b in bureau.
KJ and KI as the ch in church.
SKJ, SKI, SCH as the sh in sham.
GJ, GI, HJ, LJ as the y in yes.

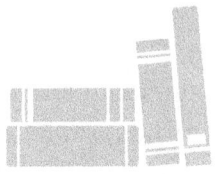

DETAILED SUMMARY OF *GIANTS IN THE EARTH*

TEXTUAL ANALYSIS

BOOK I—THE LAND-TAKING—CHAPTERS 1-3

A caravan is pushing through the tall grass of an immense prairie that seems to have no end. At the head is a stocky, broad-shouldered man closely followed by a boy of nine. Behind him an ox team is slowly drawing a wagon. Trailing this is a second wagon to which a thin cow is tied.

High on the first wagon sits the mother. A pretty little girl leans asleep against her. On her other side a seven-year-old blond boy peers steadily forward. Per Hansa is moving his family from Minnesota to the Dakota Territory where he is sure to build a fine house, make a name for himself, and thereby convince his wife he was right when they first sailed from their beloved Norway. The wife's name is Beret. The older son is Ole. The younger is Store Hans (meaning big Hans), and the little girl's name is Anne Marie. Rosie is the cow.

The family had started in the company of others but after a breakdown of their old wagon they were alone. Because the trail had vanished during a wet, drizzly spell, they became lost. To recover the trail is a matter of life and death. The bright daylight turns to gold, to red, and then to the deeper tones of violet. "Did you ever see anything so beautiful?" Ole asks his mother.

Per, who always wants to push on, is reluctantly forced by the chill of the night to call a halt. Preparations for the night proceed quickly. Each member has his chores. There is no food but a bowl of porridge for each and a little milk for the children. At the end of the meal the little girl, in her tiny voice, repeats her customary "Thanks to Thee, our Lord and Maker."

The night wears on but Per Hansa cannot sleep. Again and again he recalls his wife's early misgivings. He knows she hasn't had a happy moment since their friends went on ahead. She too lies awake. Finally Per finds the North Star, takes a bearing with his watch, slips on his pants, and heads west. He ought to be able to find the little hillock he had seen in the twilight.

He is overjoyed when he reaches it and smells the ashes of a recent camp fire. It is near a creek he was hoping to locate. His foot strikes a strange object, which proves to be a piece of meat, unquestionably one of Hans Olsa's big mutton legs. The trip back to the caravan is fast. That night he and Beret are happy again.

Shortly afterwards they catch up with the others who had driven in their stakes and begun their settlement. One sod house was already complete and others were well on the way. When Per and his family arrive, everybody rejoices. A white cloth is spread on the grass and the settlers sit cross-legged and pass the bacon, dried mutton, and flatbröd with cheese and butter. The men know what to do with the "Sunday bottle" and a dram glass. Per Hansa is in seventh heaven but Beret, his wife, looks over the stove on the open ground, the lone chair with a basin of water on it, and into the tent with its crossbeam sagging under the weight of all the family clothes. Is it for this she has come so far, so terribly far?

A shiver goes through Per as he guesses her mood, but he soon recovers, and in a burst of enthusiasm suggests that they go to see their new land, which the first-comers had laid out for him.

He and Tönseten, another of the men, set out at a fast clip. They quickly reach the highest point, where the whole wide prairie can be seen. The view is especially beautiful. Suddenly Per notices a small depression in the ground. He picks up a queer-shaped stone and then recognizes the hollow as an Indian grave. He and Tönseten go back to the others who are following and decide that since they have already crossed the line between Per's land and the next, the caravan should stop. The families should build close together.

The next morning, after Per has left for the land office in Sioux Falls, Beret catches some of the boys' joy in the new location. They have much fun unloading the wagons and arranging a bedroom in the big wagon, which seems spacious when the gear and equipment have been removed. However, when her sons announce with great glee their own discovery of the hollow in the hilltop, she fails to share their enthusiasm for arrowheads.

When Per comes back with the deed in his pockets, his spirits are at their highest. He whirls Beret off her feet. He is so tender, loving, and cheerful that she tries to choke off her fears. He has brought back ten sacks of potatoes. They are to go into the ground at once. There would be potatoes to eat and potatoes to sell. There would even be enough for a pig when there was money to buy one. The building of the sod house could wait. There was plenty of time, the whole summer and more, before the new baby was due.

Per stretches his twelve-hour work day to fifteen. His enthusiasm for farming infects the boys and even Beret. The building of the sod house is an extra, after-supper, job. The house, Per has decided, should be large, one room for the family, another for the animals. At first Beret is shocked. How can civilized people share a house with animals? But then she thinks how comforting Rosie can be.

On a side trip in search of timber, Per meets the Trönders, Norwegians from the town of Trondhjem. The Trönders tell Per much about the Indians, who had a permanent colony not too far away and who made yearly trips west to Nebraska. More than likely, Per Hansa thought, his own property lay directly on their trail. This information Per is careful to keep from his wife.

When their food supplies run low and the land has not yet brought forth its produce, the whole colony gathers together in an effort to solve the shortage. A trip, sixty or seventy miles long to the nearest town, for supplies, is decided upon. All the men leave but Per, who is elected to guard the women and children.

One day, when he is returning from the fields, he hears cries from Store Hans: "People are coming! Wagons!" They are aghast when the "people" turn out to be Indians who keep coming closer and closer. Finally the Indians unhitch their wagons and set free their ponies on Per's hillock. Per sends the boys to warn the others, who soon gather at the partly thatched house. Per insists that together they try to behave normally.

Later, when the small group is finishing the evening meal, a cow is seen heading across the fields straight for the Indian wagons. Almost immediately, the other three cows are racing behind her. They cannot be stopped. The women whose husbands are away begin to cry. They know their cows are gone, and with them, the children's main food. Beret loses patience with her husband and harsh words pass between them, especially when Per, taking one of the boys with him, sets out for the Indian encampment. He feels he must save the cows.

The man and the boy reach the hilltop where they find the Indians a peaceful but dour lot, squatting around their fire. Per chooses the Indian whom he thinks the brightest and tries out his few words of English. He is not understood but finally after much pantomime, Per realizes he is going to be able to lead home the cows.

As he is about to leave, Per notices that one of the Indians has a horribly swollen hand. He suspects blood poisoning. The Indians agree to let Per try to help. Per sends for Beret who returns with clean white cloth (her best apron), pepper, and whiskey. The couple minister to the sick man throughout the night. It is daylight when they return home happily together. After three days, when the sick man seems to be out of danger, the Indians break camp, but not before they insist on giving Per one of their ponies as a token of gratitude. The boys name the pony "Injun."

CHARACTER ANALYSES

Per Hansa.

He is a young pioneer who speaks but few words of English and is charged with the spirit of adventure. He left the old country when he felt the life of a fisherman, no matter how successful, was too constraining. His animation and daredevil courage made him popular with men. He had been something of a gay blade with the ladies until he met Beret, whom he loved at once and never stopped loving till his last breath. She loved him as devotedly. She was already pregnant when they were married.

Per was also persuasive. He stood up to her parents, who urged the couple to stay in the land of their forefathers. The enticements which were offered Per to stay were exceptional. Per was stubborn and resisted, almost unreasonably, all entreaties, including those of his wife.

They landed first in Canada, then joined Norwegians in Minnesota where they barely eked out an existence. When some of Per's friends decided to try their luck farther west, Per was once more carried away with enthusiasm. They had next to nothing saved for such an adventure. A newly acquired shrewdness and his native wit helped Per get together a caravan. It was grossly inadequate, but under the influence of his combination of foolhardiness and courage, the family set out. The children idolized their father. He was stern with them. He expected them to obey and they did. They also knew he liked a bit of fun.

Beret.

This slight, wiry woman is Per's loving wife. She could not control her love for him. Her mind never won over her heart. A refined, gentle, and intelligent girl, she had no desire to exchange her parents and her comforts for the wilderness. She prayed to God that her husband would abandon the idea of emigrating. When God did not interfere in Per's plans, she was certain that God was punishing her for her first sin with Per. Her life was an atonement she could not and did not wish to avoid. It was impossible for her not to love Per.

Her children were his children. No sacrifice was too great for them. She was hard working in spite of her delicate ways. Cleanliness, even on a water-rationed caravan, was next to godliness. Her children learned their prayers. She told them the Bible stories. She read to them and taught them their letters. Like Per she was stern with them. Although she was not so fun-loving as their father, they knew she was kind and sympathetic. Beret was continually frightened by the unknown. The wildness of the prairie terrified her. She worried about food, about money, about the children's health. But most of all she worried about what unexpected thing her husband might do next. She resented his high spirits. She regretted when his generosity went out to others, sometimes at the expense of his own family. She realized she had a duty to restrain him. In this she was persistent.

Tonseten.

There is so much conversation in this book that the characters seem to be "on stage" in a swift succession of scenes. In these, Tönseten plays the role of a comic. Physically, he is a "mister five-by-five." His beard is not only red, but pointed. He literally leads with his chin.

He is funny because he is so self-important. He is unaware of the extent of his self-conceit. When he has a bit of news, when he knows something the other fellow doesn't know, his sense of his own value becomes boundless. He bursts with excitement. He can't stand still. He almost stutters and his beard chops up and down.

Finally he is ridiculous because he thinks he has a way with the girls. He plays Romeo to all of them. He tosses out sweet endearments. He suggests a stolen kiss. He flatters with a sly wink. To most he is a silly old fool. But his fat wife adores him. She appreciates his sense of fun and realizes how lonely his life is (they have no children). She never blames him and sometimes even looks the other way, because after all, she knows he is harmless.

Kjersti.

(Pronounced Church-sti.) This plump woman is Tönseten's cheerful wife. There is not a frightened bone in her strong body. When the other women of the settlement are on the verge of hysteria, Kjersti can be counted on to save the moment. Her humor is somewhat coarse, but she is as God-fearing as any of her pioneering sisters.

Herself childless, she is adored by the children in the settlement. She is the one who can afford to spoil them with a succulent morsel. She is always ready when their mothers send them running to her for some urgent need. Generous to a fault, she is unhesitating in her willingness to help. There was little to prairie life that she really minded. She had, however, one strong dislike—Indians. She exaggerated in her mind their outrages. Not a day passed but she was on the lookout for them. Otherwise she took life calmly.

Comment

Influences.

At the very outset of any comment on Rölvaag it is important to call attention to the two major historic influences on Western man's thought—the Hebraic and the Greek. Rölvaag achieved a synthesis of these two divergent viewpoints in a way that was new in American fiction. From the Greeks the early Norwegian settlers borrowed their ideas concerning education, which to them meant reading. What they read, however, was Hebrew literature. The stories of the Old Testament figured greatly in their lives. The pioneers in *Giants in the Earth* thought of themselves as taking part in a great Exodus like that of the Hebrews from Egypt. At one point they called their settlement Goshen. Joseph and Benjamin, David and Goliath are familiar names. God is almighty.

This Hebrew concept is balanced in Rölvaag's story by the Greek idea of *hubris,* which suggests that man should not set himself up as a little god or tempt his fate. Many times the homesteaders tempted fate. Per Hansa's great strength and self-confidence occasionally made him forget the wisdom of the ancients. He is a typical Westerner, a little "Jewish" and a little "Greek." When Rölvaag mixed in a dash of Norwegian humor, the amalgam was complete.

Rölvaag's compulsion to write was primarily caused by the conviction that he could best serve his new nation by urging his countrymen to preserve the folkways of the Old World. He wanted to counteract some of the raw idolatry of material things that was sweeping America at the beginning of the century. In his criticism of this materialism Rölvaag was aligning himself with other American writers, who were his spiritual contemporaries.

Writing The Book.

At the same time, Rölvaag knew that to get his book published he would have to please the Oslo book companies. The audience whose acceptance he sought would be the same as Bojer's. The critics and members of the literary clubs of the old Scandinavian city could still make or break his book. He would have to appeal to them as well as to Norwegian-Americans. Having two audiences at the same time puts a writer in a most difficult artistic position. He planned the actual writing of his book in a way that he thought would solve the problem.

He asked and received a sabbatical year from his professorship at St. Olaf. The president of the college arranged a substantial loan. Then Rölvaag took himself with his wife and children at the beginning of the summer to a small lakeside cottage in the Minnesota woods. Here he began to write. In the fall, according to plan, he sent the family back to civilization while he pushed on with the manuscript until the cold became too severe. It was during these lonely weeks that Bojer arrived in America, and was widely feted. St. Olaf's was included in his tour, but in his letters to his wife Rölvaag makes no mention of Bojer. The trip his rival was making and which had been well advertised received not a line among: "I wrote two hours last night . . . tried hunting this morning and failed . . . wrote for an hour and a half after lunch . . . I played solitaire . . . I called it a five-hour day."

During this initial period he was confident of success. He believed he was doing an excellent job. Although the writing tired him, it gave him an exuberance he had never experienced. The story developed quickly. His greatest concern was for the authenticity of his details. When he was in doubt he asked his wife to verify his facts. He took pains with questions about the land offices where the homesteaders went for their deeds and with the limitations on claims, stakes, quarters, and sections. He worked over exact descriptions of land markers. "Every little peculiarity," he wrote, "of dress, of manner of speech, what are these but symbols of something underneath?"

The second half of his writing plan was to finish the book in Norway. He thought it essential for the success of the book that he should establish personal contact with his Norwegian audience. On arrival in Oslo he hid himself away in a furnished room and began to write. "Solitude?" he wrote, "of course any creative artist needs that. He seeks the highways of life to take his pictures; he looks for the most hidden byways to develop them. . . ." His privacy was soon invaded because he discovered that the Norwegians were as interested in the American professor as he was in them. He was invited to be a guest speaker at Oslo University. He was entertained by formal professional and literary societies and clubs. He met Bojer in his home. There he was delighted to learn, as was his host, that their two books were so different that neither had to worry about the common theme. One engagement followed another. An audience was arranged with King Haakon, who later made him a knight of St. Olaf.

Under the strain of a social load that he refused to let interfere with his writing, Rölvaag's health broke. He suffered weak spells which were attributed to his continuing heart trouble. As a result the book progressed slowly. He said he was "sailing on a tack." He was in a rewriting and revising stage that was discouraging. He was doubtful of the quality of the book. Nevertheless, before he left in the late spring for a visit to the family home at Rölvaag, Oslo's most respected publisher had not only accepted the manuscript but the firm's sales manager had given a sumptuous dinner in his honor. It was then that Rölvaag first contemplated an English translation.

Giants In The Earth And American Literature.

From the author's intentions and from the circumstances of the writing of the book. *Giants in the Earth* could hardly be expected to fit nicely into the mainstream of American fiction. Regardless of the acclaim that it first received from American critics and public, it was, and has remained, something of a "sport" in the American literary family.

Rölvaag lacked the "spiritual conservatism" of Willa Cather. *My Antonia* of 1918 was followed by more books. Her characters were people of stability and of gentility. Her art was so simple it sometimes seemed contrived. Her *Death Comes for the Archbishop*, an immediate best seller, appeared the same year (1927) as *Giants in the Earth*, which was neither simple nor contrived nor gentle.

Nor did Rölvaag's realism follow the trend that Frank Norris was said to have begun with the naturalism of *McTeague*. It is true that the insipid sentimentality that Norris revolted against is also completely absent from Rölvaag. Otherwise the writing of the two men affords slight comparison. Norris' McTeague is a man of great strength. So is Rölvaag's Per Hansa. But McTeague is stupid. Per Hansa is not. McTeague is a slave of environment. Per Hansa is motivated by the personal forces within him. The sick fleshiness of Norris' naturalism is in Rölvaag a healthy earthiness that recognizes in no uncertain terms that romance plays a part in reality.

There is a deep love between Per Hansa and his wife Beret, but these two figures are not stylized romantic types. They are individual human beings. The development of their personalities is very carefully and objectively worked out. In one of his letters Rölvaag wrote concerning Beret, "I am struggling with an insane woman." At another time he said, "The lines in her face matter little; how they came there is important."

Rölvaag's *Giants in the Earth* challenged specific classification. Here are some excerpts from the intial reviews:

"If it is not quite an epic novel, it strikes the epic note." (Isabel Paterson, *N. Y. Herald Tribune,* May 29, 1927.) "*Giants in the Earth* is a moving narrative of pioneer hardship and heroism, told with such obvious veracity that it makes almost all other tales of the Western frontier seem cheap." (R. M. Gay, *Atlantic's* Bookshelf, September 1927.) "There is a memorable simplicity and vigor about his story which place it in a class with the few really fine novels." (D. L. Mann, *Boston Transcript,* August 13, 1927.) "This seems to me much the fullest, finest, and most powerful novel that has been written about pioneer life in America." (Walter Vogdes, *Nation,* July 13, 1927.) "An amazingly simple yet forceful and dignified piece of work. Its simplicity is not a structural one, its power is not the power of restraint, its dignity is far from existing in its style." (*New Republic,* August 10, 1927.) "There can be small doubt that those who know books critically will appreciate *Giants in the Earth;* it is to be hoped that it may also reach that greater public which does not so know them, yet often, fortunately, responds with eagerness to the best." (*Outlook,* July 29, 1927.) In 1928 *Giants in the Earth* went into its forty-first printing.

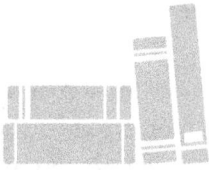

GIANTS IN THE EARTH

TEXTUAL ANALYSIS

BOOK I: THE LAND-TAKING - CHAPTERS 4-6

....

During the summer Per Hansa's neighbors watch him put more and more acreage under cultivation, and they envy his strength. His wife, on the other hand, fears that his yearning for more and more is excessive, even ungodly. She believes that for all his work he will not be able to change the raw wild prairie. Afraid to have her baby in a snowbound sod hut, she wants to return to civilization, at least for the winter. Although she plans a departure in her own mind, she postpones telling her husband.

One Sunday, after a lively tramp with the boys who wanted to show their father several ponds that were teeming with wild ducks, Per sends them home and returns by a different route. Trudging along on what he believes to be one of Hans Olsa's boundaries, he comes across a land stake. It is well-made, comparatively new and well driven into the ground. He is shocked to find it marked "O'Hara." Very sobered, he hastens along to another boundary, Tonseten's. Here he finds another stake marked "Joe Gill." Confused and angry, he hastens to his own quarter portion but finds no more markers. When he gets home, he is cross and disagreeable towards his family. Beret is frightened by this unusual mood of his. Next morning, before dawn, he is off again without saying where he is going. When he comes back, he is secretive and gruff. Later that day Beret discovers the stakes in the barn where he had obviously hidden them. She is horrified that Per should have pulled up land stakes, no matter if they bore strange and outlandish names. In Norway, where Beret came from, there was no darker crime among the peasants than to meddle with another's land stakes. What had happened to Per? Her knowledge of his crime gnaws at her very soul. She becomes numb when later she watches him burn the stakes, which he had carefully splintered and spoken of as old bits of kindling.

Later in August, the Irish arrive. When they first see them, the Norwegians, in a desire to be friendly, go over to the spot where they have camped on the boundaries of Hans Olsa's and Tonseten's land. When the settlers discover the newcomers' intention to stay, their mood changes and they hold a council. Hans Olsa, believing that the Government land office at Sioux Falls could straighten out any mistakes, urges caution even though he and Tonseten have their property deeds. Early the next day the men return to the Irish camp, where it soon becomes obvious that the Irishmen's legal papers are not to be produced. The rough and surly campers seem to be counting on the stakes to convince the Norwegians that the land is theirs. When the stakes are not found, a fight ensues, at the end of which Hans Olsa lifts one of the men, who had been threatening with a sledge hammer, high over the crowd and smashes him into a wagon. Next day the Irish move on. It is not long after the Irish have left that Per Hansa admits the story of the stakes. Most of the settlers compliment him on his quick thinking. Hans Olsa agrees but reminds Per that he acted impetuously and that had God not been on his side the event would not have ended so satisfactorily. Beret continues to be shocked. She considers her husband's admission sinful bragging. He did wrong. That O'Hara and Gill had planted the stakes without proper deeds was wrong, but their wrong did not justify his wrong. She is sick with disillusionment.

Her brooding continues and reaches serious proportions as the late fall and winter set in. Even the children notice how silent she is and forgetful even to the point where she mislays things. Once when Per is away and the boys get embroiled in some boyish scrap she lashes out against them in a wild, uncontrolled way. She raises a welt on Store Hans which is later noticed by the boy's father. Store Hans, although he is the younger, is worried about his mother and so keeps silent.

By December the snow forces all indoors. Tempers grow edgy. Per tries to keep control of himself but Beret's morbidity is challenging. More and more he sends the children over to the neighbors'. He fails to realize that Beret's innermost being needs their company no matter how disconcerting they are. She is sure God is about to punish her. She is certain she will die in childbirth and empties the big chest of her great-grandfather so that Per will at least have a coffin ready for her.

On Christmas eve, after the children have been rushed off and Sorrina and Kjersti have come to help, Beret's pains begin. Her wailing brings tears to Per's eyes as he passes back and forth outside the hut. He nearly goes out of his mind. He falls face down in the snow. At one point Beret calls him in and tells him: "I am leaving you tonight." He tries to comfort her. He goes outside again. The women, who are fearful for Beret's life, are unable to find him although he is but a few feet away.

Finally the baby is born. Per is at first unable to understand the good news. He decides to call the boy Peder Victorious. The unusual name seems fitting even if somewhat arrogant. The women suggest the boy be baptized immediately. They are afraid that in their ignorance they have handled the mother and the baby too roughly. Per seeks out Hans Olsa, who at first ridicules the idea that he should perform the christening, but after he is assured that an emergency exists, he consents. After he has read the service from the hymn book and said the prayers, Beret and the infant fall into a deep sleep. Then the others, sitting around the table, enjoy their coffee and celebrate a memorable Christmas.

CHARACTER ANALYSES

Per Hansa

In this section Per Hansa's character undergoes a subtle change. Although we still find him restless, boisterous, and carefree, we are aware that he is developing a certain cunning and craftiness. He is not only a charmer but a salesman. His salesmanship is superb when, on a trip to town with the men, he manages to swap some of his potatoes for a widow's hens. By the end of the encounter, during which he enjoys a bit of harmless flirtation, he gets a fine rooster and a hearty free meal besides.

On this same trip which he enjoys immensely, he buys supplies with considerable care, We realize he has planned each purchase. Although his youthful recklessness returns momentarily and he extends his credit too far, we recognize the wisdom of what he is doing. For example, he mystifies the others by buying net twine. They laugh at him. Does he think he is still a Lofoten fisherman? He has the last laugh, however, when later he nets river fish and snares wild ducks. The neighbors are quite willing to share in the results of his foresight.

Another side of his nature is also dramatized on this trip. In the store he lowers his voice and is bashfully secretive when he buys some gaudy calico for Beret. It takes further resolution to buy other surprises for her - some thread and pieces of ribbon. Then he buys, still timorously, some white cotton cloth and then, what he knows will please her, some sweet oil for the baby that is to come. Minutes later, he compensates for his shyness and noisily passes around his whiskey bottle. It is customary among Norwegians, when you buy a bottle, to offer your neighbor a taste. They are all buying bottles. And the storekeeper thinks he owes them a little extra to keep their good trade.

Per never for a moment ceases to love his wife, but during the last month of her pregnancy, when the weather forces him to be idle, he moodiness drives him to the breaking point. Her despondency and melancholy worry him. He loves her but doesn't understand her. In his desire to help her he makes matters worse. Once he flares up in anger and rushes from the house. He confides in Sorrina, Hans Olsa's wife, that, if he had stayed at home, he might have hit her.

Beret

In this last part of Book I some readers may find Beret as difficult to understand as her husband did. Rolvaag struggled with his delineation of her character. At this point she is deliberately portrayed as a mixed-up person. At the outset of the book, she was pictured as a delicate woman who yearns for her homeland, its customs and folkways. Later, as each day brings new hardships, her despair deepens. She turns inward and tries unsuccessfully to find comfort in Norse Protestantism. She finds only a stern God. He governs, and it is useless to struggle against Him. As she stares at the monotonous prairie that surrounds her on all sides, she is convinced that if God had ever wanted to people it, He would have done so long ago. She shrinks from it in disgust. The tall grass suffocates her, and she feels God is punishing her. After the **episode** of the stakes, about which her husband no longer feels any guilt, she fears not only the consequences of her own sins but his too. Her thoughts spin a larger and larger web of terror.

Sometimes she blames herself and sometimes she blames the prairie. Its desolation, she feels, calls forth all the evil in human nature. She believes she sees the other settlers losing their Old World decency. She is shocked by their unawareness of the ways in which they are changing. Material things become unreal to her. She gets so she can't talk to the neighbors, who notice a strange, unnatural look in her eyes. When she most needs their visits, they stay away and her melancholy increases.

At the same time she feels sorry for the others. There are times when she makes an effort to be sociable. She says to herself: "It is only I who have sinned." When she sees a new caravan slowly making its way across the prairie, she sends the boys to make offers of help. She has compassion for someone else who "has been led astray."

The children, too, are affected by her depression and changeableness. She is often sharp with them - punishes them and makes them read and study their lessons. She frightens them and yet, when one of them shows anxiety and is tender with her, she is grateful and pleasant. "Don't worry about me - just run along."

Her fearful fancies are hardest for Per to bear. She believes she must drink the cup of wrath God has handed her. As her mood darkens, she becomes careless about her person. Per's

Beret who had been such a stickler for cleanliness becomes more and more disheveled. She forgets to comb her hair. These changes frighten the man who is, for all outward purposes, so fearless. Most of the time he treats her like a child, but once in an impatient moment he scolds her and speaks sharply. She reacts by spending a long time in the barn by herself and comes back clean, tidy, and wearing a complete change of attire. She appears almost radiant to him and he is immediately happy and encouraged. His mood is contagious and she has a loving impulse to grasp him to her. However, to the sorrow of them both, her joy quickly subsides and unspeakable misery wells up in her eyes.

The Boys

Rolvaag's portrayal of children is one of the most appealing aspects of the book. The two boys are manly, courageous, and resolute, and at the same time boyish, untamed, clumsy, inquisitive, and in need of affection. Ole, the older, is the stronger, but Store Hans is the quicker. Ole is the more responsible and can be counted on to finish a job, but since Store Hans is more of a thinker he is often talked to as the older. Both of them have a bad habit of swearing. They have worked with men enough to overhear what comes out when things go wrong. For this they are continuously punished by their mother. They are also punished for fighting with each other, but their father usually doesn't interfere because he knows that within minutes they will be friends again. With their father they try hard to be grown up. Sometimes he insists on work when they would rather be off exploring something new. In the prairie wilderness there is always something new even if their mother sees only endless monotony. Their attitudes to their mother are slightly different. Ole classifies her when he says, "Only girls and women get scared." Store Hans, on the other hand, sees her as a mystery he wishes he could understand.

Hans Olsa

Everything about him is of unusual size. Not infrequently he looms up in the story like a mountain. When he is "on stage," other personalities seem to shrink. He is self-sufficient and unchangeable. When something new occurs, he is slow to perceive it, but once having grasped an idea, he is tenacious. He walks around a situation, decides what is right and what is wrong, calls for action, but then every surprisingly and humanly, adds: "We'll keep the women out of this." He doesn't want any "ands," "ifs," or "buts." He believes justice is simple and is worth fighting for. When this is the case, fire comes into his eyes and every pound of him goes into the struggle.

Sorrina Olsa

Here is an adventurous woman who is well suited to her husband. She is neither small nor frail. She has a great faith not only in the Lord but in people - men, women, and children. She is all goodness. She supplements her husband's energy and strength with a bright intelligence. She thinks fast and accurately - and sometimes intuitively because she believes that "the heart, too, has its reasons" (as the seventeenth-century French writer Pascal said). She is first a wife, then a mother, but underneath remains a tender girl who can cry over a cow. Tears don't interfere, however, with her work. When Beret's baby is due, she is willing to take over but has the wit to know she will need help. She calls on the childless Kjersti and directs her. To these two women Per Hansa must be forever grateful.

Comment

| **Existentialism**

In 1927, when *Giants in the Earth* first appeared in the United States, existentialism was not the "popular" philosophy it is today. Rolvaag would never have called himself an Existentialist. He would not, however, have objected to the label because he was an admirer of the Danish philosopher Soren Kierkegaard, who has since been called the father of existentialism. Kierkegaard died in 1855.

It is a compliment to Rolvaag that he recognized the value of this philosopher who was so far ahead of his time and who is so meaningful to so many today. Kierkegaard's followers, the French Sartre and the German Heidegger, who are the most widely known existentialists of the modern world, thought and wrote under circumstances not very different from Rolvaag's. Recent history explains the analogy. Sartre reflects the oppressions suffered by those Frenchmen who resisted the German occupation in the Second World War. Sartre's teacher, Heidegger, was surrounded by the wretchedness of the Germans after the First World War who faced crisis after crisis of hunger and self-respect when they were at once surrounded by, and isolated from, unfriendly and emergent neighbors. Rolvaag's immigrants had to undergo the same crises of hunger and isolation in a strange and unfriendly land.

Rolvaag read widely in Kierkegaard and was greatly influenced by him. As a Scandinavian he was culturally closer to Kierkegaard than was either Heidegger or Sartre. He departs from his mentor but not to the extent that the German and Frenchman do. Not just in time but temperamentally Rolvaag was closer. All four men were reacting to the philosophy of the eighteenth-century "enlightenment" and "age of reason." All four wanted to get away from complicated abstractions and get back to the real concerns of men as men and not men as brains. Kierkegaard was so firm in this belief that he was even called a "romantic." Rolvaag has also been called this. The mistake is easier to understand with Kierkegaard because of his having lived during what is generally thought of as the romantic period. Neither man was sympathetic to the chaotic emotionalism of romanticism. Both had too keen an insight into basic, unchanging human nature.

The debt that Sartre and the contemporary, existentialists acknowledge to Kierkegaard is contained in their insistence on maintaining Kierkegaard's preoccupation with the self. This stress on the importance of the individual does not make them romantics because it should be remembered that the concept of the uniqueness of man was but one of the many facets of romanticism. Modern philosophy may not be preoccupied with the self to the extent that Kierkegaard (and later Rolvaag) was because concentration on the self seems to many to be a waste of time. Others within the existentialist group feel that this indifference to self is a cause of much ethical floundering in people today.

Kierkegaard's emphasis on self had a very practical aspect. His aim was to make people fully conscious of themselves and their potentialities. Like many school teachers, he said to people: "You are not producing up to capacity." He was the enemy of self-complacency. This attitude is echoed very strongly in Rolvaag. Rolvaag felt that the second generation of American immigrants, partly because of their material successes and partly because of their separation from their own historical culture, were becoming over complacent. In *Giants in the Earth* he wrote a story of men and women who were subject to this danger. Like

Kierkegaard, he desired to shock men into an awareness of the emptiness and pretentiousness of their lives.

Per Hansa, Rolvaag's **protagonist**, never forgets his own identity. He knows exactly what he wants. He is his own flesh and bones. He is alive at the moment. Being alive, to him, is a process that extends from the past into the future. His existence is not a state of being, but a movement. Every moment contains the future. If the meaning of "future" is not limited to the immediate future, but the entire future, in other words, the eternal, then each moment contains eternity. It is this dynamic aspect of man that Kierkegaard stressed and Rolvaag reiterated in *Giants in the Earth*. It is this positive attitude that admits "believers" in eternity into the existentialist movement. If you don't believe in eternity, then the moment of now that follows the past becomes nothing, and we have, as Sartre points out, a view of man's nature as being meaningless. There is an existentialist for every shade of difference between these contrasting philosophies. Kierkegaard was a "believer," as was Rolvaag.

To return to the flesh-and-blood picture of Per Hansa, it can be said that since Per was not too concerned as to whether God (another name given to the eternal) exists or does not exist, but since he never doubts his own existence, he was an existentialist according to the definition of all existentialists, Christian or atheist. Per knows that he passionately loves a woman and that his whole existence is engaged in that love, and that because of this, or as a result of this, life is not only real but wonderful.

Just as Rolvaag internalized his philosophy in his fictional characters, so Sartre and other modern existentialists stress the personal side of life. These men make us realize how wise the medieval English philosopher Roger Bacon was when he said, "A singular thing is more noble than the universal." When we repeat, in the words of the eighteenth-century English poet Pope, that "the proper study of mankind is man," we mean man, not as the species, but man the person.

Since the "self" is naturally an elusive subject of study, existentialists recommend the contemplative rather than the introspective approach to self-awareness. Rolvaag's contemplation of himself and his fellow immigrants produced a story that is an illustration of the meaning of life. Per Hansa's whole life was a continuous asking of, and response to, the question, "What is the purpose of life?" When a man asks that question, then that man exists. Rolvaag agrees with Kierkegaard when he said: "Men don't know what it means to exist."

Rolvaag, a man who arrived in America without a dollar in his pocket, also knew that you can't have thought until you have life. He also realized that you can't really live until you have faced up to the fact that some day you are going to die. Death is an actuality of life. Until you have confronted death physically or spiritually, you can't really be said to be alive. Per Hansa in the end meets death magnificently because he regards death as the price to be paid for life, an honest and fair price at that.

In one of the letters to his wife from Oslo, Rolvaag wrote: "To live a full and rich life is up to the individual." Away from home, he was looking back at his associates at the college, his students, his connections with the Lutheran church, his family and neighbors, most of whom were first- or second-generation Norwegian-Americans. His respect for them was at a low ebb. He was a frequent lecturer and occasionally a lay preacher. He wasn't always popular because people don't want to be told of their self-complacency even if it is the truth. Earlier in life Rolvaag had given serious consideration to becoming a Lutheran minister. He had not done so because he was too much of an idealist. He blamed the complacency of the church-goer on the church organization. This attitude is reflected in Beret, Per Hansa's wife, who sometimes failed to keep her opinions concerning her neighbors to herself. His popularity as a college professor suffered from the same outspoken attitude.

Rolvaag only succeeds as a preacher or teacher of existentialism, by which he would have meant having a wide-awake attitude toward life, when he personalized his sermon or lecture through fiction. When the same old advice is spoken over and over again it becomes mere ritual and is no longer heard. Rolvaag was afraid of ritual because he saw that truth suffered when it was generalized. He embodied his text in a story about people, people of the same background as his Norwegian-American audience. By mating the hardworking, enthusiastic, pleasure-loving, materialistic Per Hansa with the contemplative, long-suffering, gentle Beret, he tells an old story in a meaningful and yet refreshing way. His thesis goes back to the book he was brought up on. "For what is a man profited, if he shall gain the whole world and lose his own soul?"

In *Giants in the Earth* Rolvaag, whose life seems to indicate that he never stopped proving to himself that God exists, tries to call these proofs to the attention of others. One of his recurring arguments is that the hunger for the eternal in the experience of every moment is a sign of the Creator in the creature. Rolvaag was always mindful that he was one of a long line of Christian witnesses to God. When the creature affirms the Creator he is testifying to his own self-respect. When the creature is aware that his creation is contingent upon the Creator he gets a whiff of the inexhaustibility and infinity of life. Per Hansa and Beret get such a whiff as it blows across the South Dakota prairie.

Rolvaag worked over his writing until he believed he made his people truly lifelike. Through Kjersti and Tonseten, through Hans Olsa and Sorrina, through the surly Irish, through the sick Indian, through the flirtatious widow, Rolvaag tries to give his readers an awareness of what it feels like to be alone. He approaches loneliness in a nonintellectual way. Although he wrote an essay on solitude, he could not say, as the Russian existentialist Berdyaev says in "Solitude and Society", "Man . . . lost the power of knowing real being . . . lost access to reality and [was] reduced to studying knowledge." Rolvaag never lost consciousness of the fact that he started life as a simple fisherman on the shore of a Norwegian cove. He learned that the present and the future run into each other. The belief in the future gives reality to the present, breathes life into it, and makes it livable.

An emigrant's life is a lonely one. Its sad notes are tragic. Yet in spite of this Rolvaag believed that the first settlers were happier than their descendants. They paid a price for their emigration, but since they had always expected to pay, they did not regret the burden. Their sons and daughters, although they did not realize it, were still paying. The price was a loss of the Old World culture which Rolvaag felt should be a stabilizing influence in their lives. He wanted them to rediscover their heritage. On this rediscovery, the development and refinement of America depended. To this end he dedicated his whole life. *Giants in the Earth* was his supreme effort.

GIANTS IN THE EARTH

TEXTUAL ANALYSIS

BOOK II: FOUNDING THE KINGDOM - CHAPTERS 1-2

In these chapters the story reaches an emotional **climax** that is developed in three distinct episodes. The first of these centers about a horrifying snowstorm. The second concerns the planting and growth of the wheat. This tale is itself interrupted by the heart-breaking interlude of the pioneer woman who has lost her mind. The last recounts the drama of the locusts.

The baby, born on Christmas day, becomes a distraction for the entire settlement. The winter keeps them in their miserable sod houses with not enough to keep them busy. The baby's name, Peder Victorious, gives them something to talk about. He is the first newcomer. His future is the subject of speculation. He may even become President of the United States. The share that every member feels she has had in the wee infant keeps up their hopes during the anxious days when the snow whirls. The lack of fuel becomes critical. They must burn hay. Anxiously they wait for a break in the weather when some of the men can organize a trip in search of fuel. Per Hansa makes a sleigh and takes advantage of whatever sunlight peeps through to train his two oxen in pulling it. Finally when the men feel they can no longer wait, they organize a caravan.

Hans Olsa's horses are the fastest. He is followed by Tonseten and then Sam Solum. Per Hansa, with his oxen, brings up the rear. In mid-morning, when they think the sun will favor them, they set out for the Tronders, where they know fuel will be available. Early in the afternoon, when they still have a long way to go, they realize a snowstorm is pursuing them and will soon catch up. A gray cloud is ominously building up. They lash their sleighs together so that when the squall envelops them they will have the comfort of being together. When the blizzard breaks with all its force, Per, in order to save himself from being dragged by the sleigh in front of his oxen, is forced to let go of his rope. Thus freed, his animals seem to go mad and for a moment in the dark, he thinks he has rushed ahead of the others. Sense of time and direction soon disappears.

After a wild dash which completely confuses Per, the animals suddenly stop. To keep himself and them from freezing Per rubs them frantically and breaks off crusts of snow that have formed. He whips them and they start up, going he knows not where, but at least at a slower pace. Fatigue seizes him and he falls out of the sleigh, but to fight drowsiness he lumbers alongside, sometimes letting them drag him through the drifts. He believes he is on his last journey, but even so, his thoughts concern Beret and the children, who he is sure are about to become fatherless. He is tempted to kill one of the beasts and wrap himself inside the warm hide. By so doing he might save himself. Even so, he cannot bring himself to murder these dumb animals that he has learned to love during their long training period. His mind begins to wander when he suddenly sees a yellow light between the heads of the two oxen. He considers it a death signal. As he lurches toward it his hand strikes a rough log and he realizes that the oxen have crashed into the corner of a house. This proves to be the Tronders', where his friends arrived two hours ahead of him.

Spring finally comes, but with it, the thaws. Per Hansa's land lies higher than the rest. He is impatient to plant his first wheat. He and the boys have worked over the seed. With an almost sensuous pleasure he lets the full golden kernels run through his fingers. He takes a chance and with the boys, Ole and Store Hans, begins to plant. He believes the ground is dry enough. Tonseten sees them at their work and hastens over from his land to say that Per Hansa is insane to think the seed will do anything but rot in the dampness. But Per persists.

The day following the planting of the last section the weather changes - first rain, then wet snow. During the night the snow reaches blizzard proportions. For two days it continues, and Per believes the devil has singled him out for destruction. Beret reminds him that God is not to blame for the disaster. Herself convinced that they deserve all the tribulations the Lord could bring, she fails to cheer him. The sun comes as quickly as the snow. It melts before their eyes and the water runs off. Even though the earth seems quite dry, Per is convinced that the seeds, some of which he has dug up, are swelling with rot. The evil trolls are set against him. He refuses to eat. He is angry and impatient with every member of the family. He stays in bed. The despair that lies so deep within him is, however, as quickly dispelled when Ole and Store Hans race each other to tell him that the wheat field is alive with thin, but strong, green sprouts!

During the warm days that follow, Per's exuberance knows no bounds. It is marred only by the arrival of a strange caravan containing a Norwegian family. The distraught and not too robust father is greatly relieved to arrive at the small settlement. The wagons had also been separated from those in whose train he had started. Like Per Hansa he had lost his way during the days when there was no sun. But he had no compass and had been wandering for days through the high grass of the boundless prairie. After the children have climbed down from the wagon, the man calls to his wife to come out. When she doesn't come, one of the boys reminds his father that he has forgotten to untie her. Hearing this, Per is shocked and hops up on a wheel to peer within. There he sees a poor woman whose wrists have been roped through the handles of a large old chest. Only a reader with a heart of stone could fail to be moved by what follows. From its vividness one would suspect not fiction, but truth.

The woman had been tied up so that she couldn't run back to the spot where a few days before she had been forced to bury one of her children, who, sickly at the outset of the trip, had not been able to survive. Sleepless with grief she had become insane, but gentle and amenable.

Here is a situation that Beret can understand. She helps the woman to the hut. She loosens her clothing, takes off her shoes and washes her face. With these kind attentions the unfortunate woman goes soundly to sleep. Meanwhile Beret goes ahead with feeding the children and their father, sends her own on errands, and brings in fresh has for bedding. Per is amazed and overjoyed at the return of his wife's efficiency. It is late before he and Beret lie down themselves and listen to the sound of the other sleepers in the big room. Their own little girl they have placed with the strange woman who continues to sleep.

At about three in the morning Beret is awakened by what she thinks is a dream in which she keeps hearing a voice calling her.

She lies awake listening, when suddenly she realizes that the woman she had put to bed is no longer there. She is so disturbed she wakes up Per at once, but fails to notice that her own little girl is missing too.

It is dawn before they find the distraught woman wandering about, clutching the sleeping child to her breast. Later that day, after making a small coffin, Per organizes a search party to find the shallow makeshift grave of the dead child. The father and mother go along. However, when they return they still have the empty coffin.

After the strange family has moved on it is not long before the wheat ripens and the neighbors gather together to reap the settlement's first wheat which Per had unwisely but nevertheless successfully planted so early. With Tonseten at the helm of the noisy but still usable reaper and the Solum boys shouting instructions to all on how to bind the sheaves, the process becomes a joyous occasion. Everybody seems happy as the women vie with one another in bringing out special treats along with the coffee they are serving to the men who work late in the fields.

The next day they have nearly finished Per's section when in mid-afternoon they see a strange dense cloud coming out of the north. (In Norway the north is the wicked place. Sinners even go down to Hell by way of the north.) These settlers who have been frightened many times before are now frightened as they never have been.

The cloud that rolls over them and rolls for hours, is a dense mass of jumping, noisy, hideous locusts. They fasten onto everything, animals and mankind. All growing things except the prairie grass, which was here before man, are destroyed. No pestilence recorded in the Bible could have been worse. Beret is so alarmed by what the Lord is doing to them that she pushes and shoves the big chest, which she had planned to be her coffin when Peder Victorious was born, in front of the sod-house door. Later Per, frantically searching for her, has to force open the door to squeeze through. He shouts and shouts but gets no answer. Beret had put the little girl in the chest, and then with the baby in her arms had crawled in herself and closed the lid. Per finds them still alive.

CHARACTER ANALYSES

Per Hansa

In these two climactic chapters the reader gets a look at this big, outgoing, headstrong young man and his faults. His weaknesses become more obvious but make him more human. One can no longer think of him as a type. As an individual he defies labels. Even though a man may appear to others to be an uncomplicated personality, that same man is a puzzle to himself, and the more he tries to know himself the more complicated he seems.

Per's most outstanding characteristic is his impatience. Impatience makes him a tragic figure; yet the reader doesn't think of Per's downfall as being caused by his tragic weakness, his impatience. One thinks of his end, which is being prepared for in these two chapters, as being caused first of all by accident, and secondly, on reflection, by the personality of his wife.

Because the winter has kept him indoors so much, Per's restlessness is understandable. It is even possible that he is glad that the fuel supply runs low and that an expedition, no matter how hazardous, must be undertaken. He welcomes the chance to do something - building the sleigh and training the oxen. In this new activity and in his mind's projection of the trip, he forgets himself, but he also forgets that the other members of the family have only more of the same shut-in life to look forward to. For Beret the monotony of the days will be worse when Per is away. To this are added her fears for him. She can't bear to look out the window to see him off. Per is to some extent aware of the loneliness in her soul, but he fails to let her know that he knows. This is his mistake.

During the snowstorm death threatens him but he is never morbid. The sucking noise of the squall reminds him of a "giant troll." Out of his racial past comes a great fear of nature. He isn't afraid for himself, but for those who will live after him, chiefly Beret and the new baby. In the baby, born at Christmas, he sees a renewal of life, a perspective inevitably the result of his faith and the faith of his forefathers. He loves, but at the same time he is "disgusted with God Almighty."

Trying to keep his seat in the sleigh against the solid blast of snow, he "stared out into the blackness. So, this was his last journey! . . . the thought only made him impatient . . . God Almighty might have waited a while longer, until they had seen how their luck would go out here and what sort of a boy Permand [an affectionate diminutive for Peder Victorious] would turn out to be . . . A strange fate, this, I'll be damned if it isn't!"

His anger at death is stronger than his fear. He wants to save the lives of the oxen. He has an investment in them. They represent his future. Without them there can be no spring ploughing. He rubs them against the cold. He calls them his "troll boys," and when he finally staggers into the hut, his first remark is: "I'm all right . . . but the oxen!"

His impatience with nature, with God, and above all, with himself is cruel. But he is too kind, one might say too soft, to be impatient with mankind, least of all with his wife and family. He can never control his impatience, but with his loved ones, if it flares quickly, he manages just as quickly to squelch it. He shouts at the boys but almost immediately he is rebuking himself for rebuking them. He tries to cover up with a joke.

His ability to laugh is part of his kindness. He wants to encourage people, especially when the going is rough. His humor is, itself, somewhat rough. He teases the Solum boys about their infrequent association with the girls in the distant settlements. He ribs Tonseten so that fat little man thinks he is cutting a figure away from home. He jostles the other wives, whose drab existence seems so cheerless. They welcome his jollity. He is being thoughtful and kind. If his humor, on occasion, is a little too coarse and his teasing is pushed a bit too far, he is unaware that he is giving the slightest offense. He is forgiven.

It is not as easy to forgive Per's actions during the period when he thinks his wheat kernels are rotting in the wet ground. When he is out of sorts and won't talk, won't eat, when he throws himself on the bed and turns his face to the wall for hours, what thoughts whirl and twist in his brain? Why is this chapter called: "On the Border of Utter Darkness"? Some of the answers involve his wife.

Beret

During the first weeks after the birth of her baby, Beret seems to have difficulty realizing that God has spared her life. Only gradually does she take any pleasure in the fact that she is having a second chance to live and that it is a privilege to take care of the small infant at her breast. But she is frightened at the strange second name her reckless husband chose for the boy.

During one of the long discussions the settlers had plenty of time to hold, while the snow enveloped their huts, the subject of surnames came up. The Norwegian customs of taking for a surname either one's father's first name or a place name seemed out of place in their new adopted land. There were too many Hans' sons, Peter's son, Olaf's sons; too many -dahls, -fjelds, -gaards, and -stads. Because Beret came from a place called Skarvholmen, jokes began to go around. How would she like to be called Mrs. Skarvholmen? The name was a subject of fun because "Skarv" in Norwegian means a cormorant - an ugly sea bird - and as an adjective, is used to describe persons of low character. Thus "Skarv" was dropped, and then later "holmen" was shortened to Holm: Mrs. Hans Christian Holm. This sounded fine to Per and still better yet was Peder Holmen - Peder Victorious Holm.

Beret didn't laugh. She was shocked that the settlers could discard the names of their fathers. "Soon they would be discarding other things. The awful spirit that ruled the plains demanded all! . . . It was a wicked thing that they were doing now! Not that it was any worse than their giving the child that terrible second name to start with; for that had been almost sacrilege! . . . . But perhaps she was mistaken after all. Perhaps it hadn't been wrong. Perhaps she was going crazy."

During the weeks that followed, while they were waiting for the spring, she said very little to her husband. He was off a good deal on trips on which he bought fur from the Indians and sold it at a high profit in Minnesota. He was proud of his success and of the money he showed her. He felt that at least she could have thanked him. Had she understood how close to death he had been more than once on these solitary trips, she would have spoken up. Better not to tell her. Meanwhile she kept her own terror at being so much alone deep within her.

When Per took to his bed during the blizzard that came after his planting of the wheat, Beret began to be more concerned about him. When she brought him some soup, he found fault with her: "For God's sake, couldn't she leave him alone? He told her he didn't want anything to eat, and wasn't that enough? . . . Well then . . . Oh, hell!"

When the sun came out and the wheat came up, he soon forgot that power from heaven that had stepped down to defeat him. He forgot that fellow (the devil) who was chasing him. He forgot the beam and the rope that had beckoned to him. Tears came to his eyes when he saw the green shoots of the wheat. Store Hans caught him blowing his nose. Per placed his hand on the boy's shoulder and asked him: "What are you going to be when you grow up?" When the boy answered that he wouldn't mind being a general, like Grant, the father said they needed a minister more. They went back to the hut together, and Per asked Beret to read from the Bible. He got more comfort out of the reading than she did.

Per was proud of Beret's behavior with the deranged woman who had lost her child. He admired her efficiency in caring for the hungry family. Above all, he loved her for being kindly and very comforting to the sick and grieving wife. Nevertheless, Per had little idea how the **episode** built up Beret's fears. She brooded over what had happened. Once she burst out to her husband, "Now you can see that this kind of life is impossible! It is beyond human endurance."

She could find no peace after the family had departed. She was divided within herself. She had been glad that her rough hut had become a comfortable home in comparison with the flimsy wagon the poor souls were forcing through the tall prairie grass. And she had to admit, too, that she was glad that the family had moved on. This very gladness, however, disturbed her. That she should be glad to be free of these lost souls was a terrible thing. It was sinful to send them, nearly defenseless, into the wilderness. Why hadn't she delayed their leaving? It was a sign that she was becoming an evil thing herself. When God had spared her life at Christmas, He had given her more time - time that she had better spend in repenting her sins. But somehow she couldn't repent. She could only fear. She wanted to cry but no tears came. Sometimes her loneliness was so great that she had a great physical need to do something for somebody. Then she would cook a special dish for the boys, who were grateful. At this Per would take heart and try to make a joke out of her usual quietness or her need to cover up the windows. But as time passed, his laughter became rarer. Her fears began to possess him, too.

When the locusts came and he nearly went crazy looking for her, and when he found her in the coffinlike chest with the little girl and the baby, her first remark was one of surprise that the devil hadn't gotten him yet. However, it was she who came first to her senses. It was Per who cried and buried his head in her lap. It was she who had to comfort him, to caress him and love him tenderly while outside the fiendish locusts crackled and crinkled across the incredible prairie.

Comment

It has become academically fashionable to look for symbols in literature. This method of criticism has been valuable and has often led to a fuller understanding and enjoyment of the work being examined. On the other hand, as Saul Bellow pointed out in *The New York Times Book Review* (February 15, 1959), this search for the symbolic can be overdone. Mary McCarthy, in an article in *Harper's Magazine* (February, 1954), arrived at the same conclusion. Depending on his background and psychological bent, any reader can find symbols in any work. *Giants in the Earth* is no exception.

When the story is exciting and the characters are easily identifiable, there seems little need for "fuller understanding" and "greater enjoyment." This book can be "felt" without mental exertion. Symbols may easily be found that suggest universal truths from specific details. Two such symbols suggest themselves: the Sea of Life and the House.

Both of these symbols are recurrent in the literature of the Western world. Both are to be found in the Greek poet Homer. It is very doubtful whether Rolvaag consciously employed them, but he uses so many metaphors concerning both the sea and the house, or home-building, that they cannot be glossed over.

On page 1, paragraph two, the sun on the prairie "threw into life waves of yellow and black and green . . . a dead black wave would race over the scene." In the next paragraph the caravan going through the grass left a track "like the wake of a boat - except that instead of widening out astern it closed in again." A little further on, the cow that was tied to the last wagon moved along "swinging and switching her tail, the rudder of the caravan."

The **metaphors** and **similes** of the sea on whose shores Rolvaag had been born and on whose waves he had played, worked, and even struggled for his life, recur with sufficient strength to remind one of Odysseus and his voyage home after the sack of Troy in Homer's *Odyssey*. Homer recounts **episodes** of disaster and shipwreck that take place on real seas that symbolize everyman's struggle through life. So in *Giants in the Earth* man fights for survival on the sea of life, but this time the sea is a boundless prairie that stretches from horizon to horizon. Like a mariner, Per Hansa in Chapter One still "looked for the north star, found it, turned about until he had it over his right shoulder . . . hurried off westward."

Later on during one of the snows, the settler curses, "'Damn the luck, that we haven't got a compass!' The words tumbled out of Per Hansa's mouth in a raging flood." "The snowflakes floated about . . . they followed no common course . . . the western sky foamed and flooded." Before the battle with the storm the men had lashed their sleighs to one another like sailors in boats trying to keep contact. Concerning Per's sleigh, Rolvaag writes that "the boat that he steered was behaving badly." At another time, the man whose wife had lost her mind had tried to "steer with a rope," when he was lost in the mists of the prairie. But the rope had been too short to make a straight line in the dust. A straight line would have meant to a sailor a straight course.

Sometimes the references to the seaman's life are pleasanter. The episode in which Per surprises his companions by buying "net twine" is followed by the story of his staying up all night to finish the weaving of the net. At one point he "had already knitted four fathoms of it." Nets could be made to snare birds as well as to catch fish. One of the boys boastfully talks of an animal as being "deader than a herring" and evokes a smile.

"How exciting they were, those little ships of the Great Plain! the prairie schooners, rigged with canvas tops, gleamed whitely as tiny specks against the eastern sky; one might almost imagine them to be sea gulls perched far, far away on an endless green meadow." Sometimes "the caravans would . . . come to anchor." Then they would be off again. "The white sails grew smaller and smaller." "Yonder drifted these folk, like chips on a current."

Single words such as "ebbing," "surging," "deep," "unfathomable" are used repeatedly. In other passages the **metaphors** are extended. When Beret watches Per go off on one of his voyages, she "watched his figure grow less and less in the dim grey light of breaking day, until at last it had disappeared altogether . . . to her it seemed as though he were sinking deeper and deeper into an unknown sea; the sombre greyness rose and covered him." At another point, Per Hansa was behaving like "a good boat in a heavy sea - as long as the keel pointed the right way, he would go on."

There are many references to the Lofoten fishing grounds, where the Tronders and Helgelanders, who became such good prairie neighbors, had for generations jealously fought each other and the sea. Per Hansa "had ridden the frail keel of a capsized boat on the Lofoten seas . . . had seen the huge, combing waves snatch away his comrades one by one, and had rejoiced in the thought that the end would soon come for him also; but things of this sort had been mere child's play . . . this was utter darkness."

Getting ready to go to another settlement, they had to "make preparations as if for a voyage to Lofoten." On another occasion, "time had simply come to a standstill! He had never seen the like, this was worse than the deadest lay-up in Lofoten."

Probably one of the most vivid **metaphors** occurs in the description of the sudden appearance of the locusts. "They came in waves, like the surges of the sea and cast a glittering sheen before them . . . the ominous wave of cloud seemed to advance with terrific speed, breaking now and then, like a huge surf and with the deep roaring sound as a heavy undertow."

Before detailed consideration is given to the symbolism of the House, it may be helpful to be reminded that the Greek word for house, oikos, plus another Greek word nemein meaning to manage, give us our word "economy." The economics that lay behind the European situations that propelled so many immigrants to our Western plains is common knowledge, extensively dealt with in history textbooks. Let us not forget these underlying facts as we review the concept of the House. Here it is also perhaps worthwhile to recall that the Homeric story of Odysseus does not begin with his sea voyage. It begins with the story of Telemachus, who had grown during his father's absence from boy to man. It was his duty to throw out the suitors who were spoiling the economy of his house. The goddess Athene is his helper. She is not only the goddess of wisdom but also the goddess of the household and the goddess of weaving. We think of Penelope's device of weaving during the day and unraveling at night. This is her way of keeping off the suitors and saving the house of her husband. Only when Telemachus leaves his home in search of news of his father does the story of Odysseus' adventures begin, in medias res (in the middle of things). The struggles of Odysseus **climax** in his return home. His appearance there in disguise allows the poet to present several stories within stories on the subjects of the building, the roofing, the marriage bed, the storage chests, and the festivals (including the account of how Odysseus and his son received their names). Not until the last book do we witness the murder of the suitors and the re-establishment of Odysseus as king in his own house.

Rolvaag tells the story of Per Hansa, a young man who leaves the house of his fathers for economic as well as other reasons. Per takes a long voyage, first across the sea and then across the prairie. He is ambitious to build a house for himself. He wants to establish his "line." Before Per reaches home, many stories within stories are told. Sometimes they are illustrated by single word **metaphors** and sometimes by longer symbols. Many concern the house, its design, its building, its roofing, its economics, its weaving, its management, its household gods, and its preservation and future.

On page 2 we see how the Norwegian immigrants had roofed over their wagon with "woven blankets that might have adorned the walls of some manor house in olden times." When they arrive at the settlement, Per exclaims, "This kingdom is going to be mine."

Chapter Two is called "Home Founding." In it is described the building of the sod house, Per's own sod house. It is to be longer than the others, two rooms, house and barn under one roof, a very special roof, too big for the local willows to span, a roof requiring a hazardous trip for lumber. "This crazy man," cries Tonseten, "will start building a tower on it, too!"

Meanwhile, Per tells his wife to "watch the royal mansion rise." When he comes back from the land office, he tells her: "Here is the deed to our kingdom, Beret grill!" He is shaking off the old country when he calls: "I can make it for you, this kingdom of ours! . . . and no old worn-out, thin-shanked, potbellied king is going to come around and tell me what I have to do about it, either."

Where he first built their sod house, a large dwelling would someday stand. "The royal mansion he had already erected in his mind . . . the palace itself would be white, with green cornices, but the big barn would be red as blood, with cornices of driven snow."

While one adversity after another postponed the building of this castle, improvements went on little by little in the sod house. For example, it was the only one that had whitewashed walls. Per was so proud that he had learned about lime ahead of the others that he forgot that the walls could be very glaring, especially when there was snow outside. The very whiteness of the hut depressed Beret; when a rich new homesteader came and boastfully talked, to Per's disgust, about building a wooden house, Beret remarked, "It would be a fine thing . . . to see a real house once more," and offered to help the man's "wife weave a few carpets." She had none of her own.

In moments of depression her "thoughts slowly began to spin; the longer they spun, the less she liked the web. . . . Beret would look at her web until her whole body trembled." As a housewife she took some comfort in the old family chest her grandfather had given her. It bore an inscription half rubbed away by age: "Anno 16___." She kept her best things in it, but then took them out when she thought a coffin was needed. Her weaving is not comparable with the fun Per had in knitting the net twine as a surprise for the boys to use in their birding expeditions.

"Could Destiny have spun his web more cunningly?" The strange name Per gave to the first baby born in the settlement, Peder Victorious, was a name with which to found a dynasty. No wonder Beret was awed, not by the babe but by his father. From her viewpoint, kings were kings by divine right. At one point when she is brooding over the skyline, we read: "A magic ring lay on the horizon . . . within this circle no living form could enter;

it was like the chain in closing the king's garden, that prevented it from bearing fruit."

Whereas Per grabbed cornices that he knew could only be Norwegian, when his oxen crashed blindly into the house, Beret's idea of buildings was very different in its nostalgia. She saw castles in cloud banks. Fairies and trolls were part of her innermost being and woven into her religion. There will be more comment later about the religion of these edda- and saga-loving people ("eddas" and "sagas" were the literature of the ancient Norsemen), who were also Bible-reading homesteaders familiar with the stories of the House of David and the very real God in whose House there are many mansions.

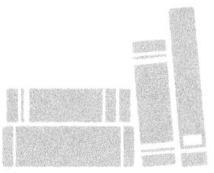

GIANTS IN THE EARTH

TEXTUAL ANALYSIS

BOOK II: FOUNDING THE KINGDOM - CHAPTERS 3-4

One June day a few years after the summer that brought the grasshoppers an old dilapidated cart drawn by a raw-boned nag is pulled up in front of Tonseten's by a man in a thin black coat. From his agile movements as he jumps down from the seat, one might say he was about forty. From his worn wrinkles, his gray beard, and from the tired expression of his eyes, one might be more apt to guess sixty-five or better. When the stranger addresses Tonseten in his native Norwegian with a favorite phrase, Tonseten is delighted and lets out something roughly equivalent to: "What the devil!: Immediately, Tonseten is sternly rebuked for swearing and Kjersti, his wife, is all of a fluster as she realizes that the supper she has on the table needs to be dressed up to be worthy of none other than a minister.

After a long grace, during the course of which the minister prays that Tonseten's sins may be forgiven, a hearty meal, and several pipefuls of what the minister calls "incense," the three become firm friends. Plans are made that he hold his first "church" service at Per Hansa's because his sod hut still has the biggest single room of the settlement. They do warn the minister, however, that Beret has become increasingly queer since the birth of Peder Victorious and that Per Hansa may have to put his wife away. Even with this knowledge, the minister wants to go ahead with his plan.

Early the next day, Tonseten is abroad summoning every settler to the service. The years had brought many new adults and more babies. The minister would perform the baptisms, and would even rebaptize those who had been christened at home. Tonseten, who, in his elected capacity as sort of justice of the peace, had at one time married a couple, and in so doing, thought that he had committed a great sin, wants the minister to remarry them, but this the minister assures Tonseten is unnecessary, especially since from this union there were three children to baptize.

Quite a crowd gathers at Per Hansa's when the service is to begin. The room is hot and stuffy, and the overflow outside is not easy to quiet down. The force of the minister and his message brings tears to the eyes of many who are grateful that this man of God has come to them. The service proceeds smoothly until it is the turn for Peder Victorious' rebaptism. At this point Beret, who has been quietly sitting in the background, pushes her way forward to stop the baptism of the boy, who is now four years old and whose playfulness is bringing smiles to the congregation as Sorrina, his godmother, carries him. She is screaming that it is a sacrilege to baptize a boy with that preposterous second name. At the command of the minister, Per Hansa lifts up his wife and carries her, kicking and struggling, out of the hut.

After the settlers have all gone back to their farms, the minister has a long talk with Per, who has grown much older in appearance. He has born a heavy cross and at first he thinks it is just too easy for an elderly minister to be glib in his advice, and to recommend "Patience" and that the Lord in His own time will restore her health. Toward Beret the minister is kindly but direct and matter of fact. She seems slightly abashed and guilty-looking, but there are no more scenes. He tells her to prepare for his return in two weeks when he will hold a communion service. He tells her how he wants the room to be arranged. The men are to build some benches. Beret's family chest, which was to be her coffin, is to serve as an altar.

From this time forward Beret seems to improve, and after the minister's second visit, Per is overjoyed to see his wife hustling about with her old efficiency, even helping him with the work outdoors. She is even singing hymns and instead of rebuking little Peder, she can't seem to find enough time to play with him. Per is tempted to take her in his arms, but he had been treating her so gently for so long through the years of her increasing sickness that he can't bring himself to treat her other than as a child, especially since the older boys have grown into such manly farm hands.

Several years pass. The colony grows. Per Hansa, despite the annual return of the grasshoppers, manages to grow more and more prosperous. His success is surpassed only by that of Hans Olsa, who of course had a head start and initial capital. Hans Olsa is most fortunate with his cattle. He developed a large herd which he lets graze without much trouble on additional outlaying land he had acquired. Hans Olsa had also built a large comfortable two-story frame house. Beret would be wistful for its expansive kitchen if she did not consider it sinful to be envious. Also, she is not sure that Hans Olsa, even more than her aggressive husband, is not taking too much thought of his new wealth instead of storing up more treasure in heaven.

Hans Olsa thinks the time has come when he can safely leave his herd up in the new field all winter if he can build an adequate shed for them. He is pushing this building to completion when suddenly, in mid-October, an unexpected snowfall comes. He is worried about the cattle and decides he must see how they are faring. The wind and snowdrifts have raised havoc with the poles and loose lumber. He finds the cattle struggling for protection on the lee side of the partly finished shed. He tries to get them around, but since this means heading into the wind they won't follow. He forces them one by one. Even though the exertion is too much for him he literally picks up the smaller beasts and carries them in. By the time he feels he must return he is wet with perspiration and shaking with fatigue and cold. Because he feels he must rest, he props himself up for warmth between two oxen. He soon realizes that his feet are beginning to freeze. He stumbles up and tries to walk up and down in his bare feet. He is afraid he will be crippled for life. As soon as the circulation begins to come back, he decides to head for home.

When he arrives there, Sorrina, who has been frantic with worry and had even tried to get over to Per Hansa's for help but had been turned back by the storm, is relieved to see him, but frightened by the trembling, weak condition of this giant among men. She gets him in bed, where her can't lie still because of an uncontrollable cough. By the next morning she realizes how sick her husband is.

Sorrina gets word to Per Hansa, who manages to get through the storm and set up more protection for the beasts about whose safety Hans Olsa is so concerned. Beret is able to get to Sorrina's so that she can help with the sick man. While the storm continues, and the drifts near Tonseten's (where the ground is lower) are estimated at twenty feet, Hans Olsa's condition worsens. The only help they can get is from an old crone who has many times administered successfully to the sick "Crazy Bridget" gets over on her snowshoes, prescribes scalding hot poultices in which she has buried a rusty crucifix, and leaves again without too much hope for the sick man's recovery.

One night while Beret is tending him and singing her hymns, Hans Olsa inquires about the storm and asks Beret if she thinks it would be possible for Per Hansa to get through to fetch a doctor. Beret shocks him by saying that he needs a minister more than a doctor. "Yes," she continues, "when the Lord's hour is at hand, man's help is of no avail; for from His wrath no man can flee! . . . what you need most of all is Communion, Hans Olsa!"

The next night Per Hansa substitutes as nurse for Beret, who has had to leave so that she can help a woman in childbirth. Hans Olsa discusses his affairs with his old friend Per and tells him what he wants done when he dies. Then he asks Per about the storm. Per, who has seen no sign of its abatement, tries to evade the subject and reassure the sick man, who almost immediately is seized with such a violent coughing spell that neither Per nor Sorrina thinks he can survive.

Back in his home the next morning, Per tells Beret the events of the night. Beret insists that he can't allow his old friend to meet death without a minister's help. Per tries to explain the impossibility of getting very far through the snow. She persists in telling him that he must try. If the Lord wants him to get through he will; if the Lord turns him back the Per will at least know he has done all in his power. At this, Per becomes angry, and when Beret puts on her outdoor clothes and some of Per's on top of these, and says she is going to get Henry Solum, to get him to do what Per won't do, he is outraged. He forbids her to move, goes out himself, and slams shut the door behind him.

Left alone, Beret trembles with fear. Shortly after she goes to the window and watches Per put on his skis. She knows how much she loves him. She can't let him leave in anger. She sends little Peder Victorious outside to his father to say she has coffee waiting for him. Per can hardly believe the boy's words. He is so grateful for them. After sending the little boy in from the cold and taking another look at the house, he leaves. From the window Beret soon sees his disappearing figure vanish completely in a whirl of snow.

The next spring, after Hans Olsa's death, some boys in search of stray cattle find Per Hansa's body propped up against an out-of-the-way haystack. His stocking cap was pulled down; his skis were beside him. So ends the novel.

CHARACTER ANALYSES

The Minister

In Chapter Three of Book II, which is the next-to-last chapter of the novel, the minister appears for the first and only time. The chapter, entitled "The Glory of the Lord," is so dominated by the minister that he becomes, even though he remains nameless, one of the book's most unforgettable figures. In one sense he is the only giant in *Giants in the Earth*. The other two possible giants, Per Hansa and Hans Olsa, both go down, perhaps on the same day. In the downfall of each the hand of the minister's inexorable God seems to intervene with almost human suddenness and willfulness.

In outline, the minister conforms to a type used by Rolvaag in his earlier novels that were never translated from Norwegian. He is a stern servant of a stern God, a God who demands that the devil and all his ways be forsaken. Only by strict adherence to God's laws can the fight against "that one" be won.

The idea that sins can be ranked, that some are more serious than others, is an ancient one. The sins of the flesh, to which all mortals are prone, are less damnable than the sins against God, which include blasphemy. Since the Norwegian settlers have a bad habit of swearing, especially when they lose patience in their struggles with the hardships of the prairie, the men's souls are blackened. In this sparsely settled wilderness there is no hint that a man is ever unfaithful to his wife. Indeed, this would be a lesser sin than greed, which is rampant.

In times of plenty as well as scarcity, when the virgin prairie soil brings forth its golden grain in rich abundance, when wealth is easy and comes with a quickness unheard of in the old country (where the status of a family hardly changes from one generation to the next), the desire for more and more material gain appears to be unchecked. Spiritual awareness is evident only when the natural phenomena of the prairie, its summer heat, its pests, its snow and wind are overwhelming. With prosperity, God is forgotten. This is the general atmosphere the minister confronts on his arrival.

Fortunately for the settlers this man of God is also a man among men. First of all he is a healthy and hungry person. He helps himself unstintingly to the bounty the prairie women put before him. They appreciate his praise. He has a soft voice and a kind smile that can turn, on occasion, into a loud chuckle. The men admire the youthful vigor of one whose beard is streaked with gray. He is a sensible man who knows something about farming, certainly enough not to offer advice that is unasked for. He grows in greatness and power before their watching eyes during his first sermon, when he preaches on the coming of the Israelites to the land of Canaan and shows them their own feelings during the lonely hours. The truth he implants remains steadfast. He is in command of the situation when Beret loses control during the baptism. His command: "Take your wife outside, Peder Holm!" is followed by quick thinking. "The air in here is close and bad for a sick person. I will talk to her afterward ... and the rest of you - please keep quiet!"

Afterwards, before he talks to Per, the minister takes time out to hold little Peder on his knee and begins to play with him. Later, the boy toddles "along beside him, hanging on to the black gown as if it were a great joke." It seems as if the minister is using this playtime to organize his conversation with Per, which he foresees will be difficult. When he does sit down with Per, he begins with sympathy and understanding: "Now tell me everything. Two can carry what one alone cannot lift. Tell me everything from the beginning."

It takes Per some time to get to the details of his troubles, but because of the minister's patience and persistence, he finally unburdens himself, sometimes crying out for help, sometimes even sobbing. He has tried so hard with so little success to help Beret. The minister looks at him with sympathy and understanding. That he is a man as well as a preacher is obvious from his words, "Take no thought for the morrow! ... remember the Lord is always near ... and now take this advice from me: From now on keep close to her; be toward her as you were during those happy days when you first got her; let your affection warm her into the understanding that it is good to be human, and lighten her burdens in every way ... and now I will perhaps stay here tonight; arrange it so I can be alone with her awhile tomorrow." So Beret's recovery begins.

Aslak Tjome

Among those who come to hear the minister preach is old Aslak Tjome. The portrait of this minor character is one of Rolvaag's best. Accustomed as the reader is to various characters who move in and out of the story, he is unlikely to forget the sparkle of this very merry Norseman.

"Old Aslak Tjome . . . brought his wife in a wheelbarrow. She had fractured her hip on the ice that spring and was still unable to walk . . . and Aslak was bringing his wife to church for this reason: he had a notion - just a notion - that if the minister would lay his hands on her, she might gain faster . . . anyhow, there was no harm in trying. . . . Aslak, with his wife in the wheelbarrow, made a funny sight; he had rigged up a high back-rest for her and fixed a seat in the barrow covered with a sheepskin rug; on this she sat like a queen on her throne. On either side of the wheelbarrow he had fastened short poles, connecting them with a rope. The woman clung to the rope with one hand; in the other she held a hymn book wrapped in a white handkerchief.

"Folks passing them stopped and laughed and offered to push awhile. 'Oh, no, thank you!' said Aslak, merrily. 'Now I can manage her alone; but it hasn't always been thus - no, indeed!' Then he laughed again as he pushed on and looked lovingly at her. She nodded and smiled laughing back at him. . . . 'You take my place and let me push for awhile!' . . . that gave them a good laugh together."

Hans Olsa

He is a solid individual, firm, clear-cut in his ideas, courageous and unchangeable. He enjoyed the company of men and the challenge of being with them. He admired Per Hansa, another big man, strong and self-reliant. Because of Per's troubles with his wife, we are prepared for a subtle change in Per's makeup. We expect no such change in Hans Olsa, whose wife, Sorrina, is a robust, fearless, and practical-minded helpmate. We are surprised, therefore, to find Hans Olsa behaving, as it were, out of character. Strangely enough, Beret is involved.

After the minister had helped Beret dispel her morbid fears and she had resumed her active life as mother and farm wife, she remained intensely religious. If God was no longer punishing her, He was still close beside her as teacher, guide, and inspiration. Her praise for the Almighty was even joyous at times. Being thankful for her blessings, she did not resent her burdens, which were either man-made or the work of the devil. Man had a duty not only to obey God's laws but also to fight the devil. From such duties she does not exempt herself, her children, her husband, or her friends. Hans Olsa, particularly, is not exempt. Therefore he avoided her when he could. He thought of her as a good woman, almost too good for such a humble sinner as he was.

Suddenly, Hans Olsa finds himself sick, with Beret for a nurse. She, who knows more about God than he does, tells him he is mortally sick. She knows all the lessons used to correct the misdemeanors of bad boys. Hans Olsa is without doubt a bad boy. Per Hansa thinks of his friend as a boy, yes but not a bad boy, certainly no worse than any high-spirited male. Beret, however, sees Hans Olsa as a sinner blacker than most, so hardened by the tough life of the prairie that he has grown unaware of his sins. She points out to him, between hymns and in an effort to be kindly, that he has indeed been striving to be more than a good father and a good provider, but that he has also become land-greedy, overambitious, over self-confident, over coarse, and even blasphemous. Per Hansa is shocked by his wife's attitude and persists in thinking that his friend is one of the most honest, most generous, most courageous giants among men, one who needs neither minister nor minister's helper to guide him into the next world. He agrees with Sorrina that the man needs a doctor more than a priest. Hans Olsa listens to Beret. She has convinced him that he needs the last rites. He asks Per Hansa to get a minister.

Per is puzzled. How could this man who was never afraid to live be afraid to die? How could this man who seemed always willing to fight for himself, fight for his family, fight for his rights and his friends' rights, suddenly lose his courage? Rolvaag doesn't answer Per's questions. It would appear that in failing to answer, the author wants the reader to look within himself for his own solution. Rolvaag, who had been close to becoming a minister himself, was above all a teacher who knew that no answer was better than a wrong answer. He makes it clear what some of the wrong answers might be.

A wrong solution might be that Hans Olsa was a coward who feared bodily dissolution or the torments of hell. Another wrong answer might be that he agreed with Beret, whose type of religion he did not admire. Still another wrong answer might be that he panicked. Rolvaag is definite in describing the calm with which the sick man settled his worldly affairs. Again a wrong answer might be that his physical weakness had become so great that his mind was affected. We can be sure that this is not the case because of his awareness of the storm and the question whether it was too severe for a man like Per to brave.

GIANTS IN THE EARTH

CHARACTER SUMMARIZATION

AND-ONGEN (ANNE MARIE)

The only daughter of Beret and Per. At the beginning of the book she is a mere toddler and is affectionately known as the "Duckling." She is put to bed, at one point, with the poor woman who buried a child on the prairie. In her insanity the woman picks up the sleeping child and wanders off with her.

ASLAK TJOME

Aslak means blacksmith. Rolvaag may have borrowed the name from Ibsen who has a character by the same name in *Peer Gynt*. The two characters are alike in name only. In *Giants in the Earth* Aslak is the good-natured peasant who brings his crippled wife to the church service in a wheelbarrow.

BERET

(Later in the novel she is called Mrs. Holm or, familiarly, Mother Holm.) The leading female figure of the novel, she is the frail, sensitive wife of Per Hansa. She represents the type of woman Rolvaag believes should never have left Norway. In real life, many women such as Beret were unable to withstand the rigors of the prairie wilderness, which in one way or another frequently took their lives. Unable to reconcile herself to the loss of the comforts of established with its cultural, religious, and social advantages, she becomes afraid. She looks upon her existence as a punishment for past sins (more imaginary than real). Her chief desire is to go back, but she is unable to do this because of her deep love for her adventurous husband, whose entire life is directed toward pioneering. When, on their first Christmas eve, with the snow almost enveloping the sod hut, she is brought to bed in childbirth, she is convinced she is about to die. Her rough but kind-hearted neighbor women manage to save her life but not her mind. In her delusion she talks to her mother who, she believes, has passed on. This is indeed true, although no word has yet arrived of her death. Beret believes that her mother wants the newly born child with her in the next world. In talking about sending it there she frightens her older children. Her husband tries to straighten out the situation by giving the child to neighbors. When this doesn't help, Per is worried he will have to send her away as a crazy woman. However, she does regain her senses, but in recovering she becomes a religious fanatic. Ironically, her firm belief in the next world brings her back to reality; yet at the end of the book this same faith drives her husband into the jaws of death.

CRAZY BRIDGET (KRAESI-BRITA)

The old Irish crone who spoke no Norwegian and only a little broken English jabbers away in a language only partially intelligible to a few of her own people. Her homemade remedies for the sick (man or beast) win her the respect of the settlement.

She trudges over on her snowshoes to Hans Olsa's bedside but fears he is beyond mortal help.

THE DANISH WIDOW

Like The Minister this character has no name but is memorable nevertheless. It is she who barters her chickens for Per's potatoes and melons. After some sharp bargaining about price, she feeds Per a hearty meal during which the two lonely souls revive their spirits with a few earthy laughs.

JOE GILL

One of the Irishmen whose strange name was on the land stakes Per pulled out. When Beret saw the letters, she asked, "Did people really have such names?"

GURINA BAARSTAD

(In Norwegian the double a is sometimes written as a single a with a little circle on top. Therefore, in some texts this name will appear as Barstad. This is usually pronounced as a sound coming between our au as in "caught" and our ea as in "earth.") She is one of the Tronders (The o with the two dots is not pronounced like any sound in English. It is closest in sound to the German o, and is sometimes printed as o: Tronders.) When Per stumbles into her hut after his battle through the snowstorm with the oxen, it is Gurina who gives him the hot milk mixed with the strong home-brewed beer. Having downed one large bowlful he wants another. Gurina later sells him a year-old heifer.

HANS OLSA

Per's old companion and Lofot-man (one who braved the winter sea on the fishing grounds at the Lofoten Islands far north on Norway's west coast, an area of the midnight sun in summer and noonday dark in winter). At the beginning of the book he is described as a man of "strength and massive build." "His loud voice led the cheerful talk; his ponderous bulk was always the centre of attention." "That man was equal to any task." ". . . he understood all the essentials."

Later in the book during the fight with the Irishman with the sledge hammer, Hans Olsa "stood for a moment as if rooted to the ground. Then, all of a sudden, the upper part of his body seemed to stretch . . . his left fist shot out and struck the man below the ear . . . the man sank in a heap. . . . Regaining his balance he [Hans Olsa] stopped, bent over, and plunged both hands into the inert heap of flesh; the next instant he lifted it high in the air and flung it bodily over the heads of the crowd. . . ."

At the end of the book this same man ". . . doesn't expect to get over this sickness . . . he just lies there and whimpers about having the minister." Nevertheless the reader continues to believe along with Per Hansa, who says ". . . As for Hans Olsa, the Lord will find him good enough, even without either minister or Klokker" (a church official having the duty partly of cantor and partly of sexton. In early Norwegian history a man too much of a blockhead to be ordained a minister was appointed Klokker. Syvert Tonseten was thus elected Klokker by the pioneers toward the end of the story.)

BRIGHT NOTES STUDY GUIDE

HALVOR HEGG

A latecomer to the settlement.

JOHN

One of the sons of the crazy woman who had lost her child.

KARL

John's mother.

JAKOB

Her frail, inefficient, and discouraged husband.

KJERSTI

A healthy counterpart to Beret, she is a strong and robust woman. Underneath an outgoing manner there lurks, however, a girlish shyness. She has to put up with a windbag of a husband but even this she does with the good grace she displays toward any misfortune. She is childless, and so she spoils the settlement children, for whom she almost always had something extra to eat. Food was one of her chief interests. When the minister showed up unexpectedly, "'Oh, my! Oh, my!' wailed Kjersti, awestricken, yet overwhelmed with joy. '... if he can only eat the stuff we have!'" Later, "... she watched the minister as he helped himself liberally to the food, and felt the blessing of it descend upon her. How kind of him to say the nice things he did about the food she had prepared!"

THE MINISTER

The man was his own best message. To him the spirit of the law was more important than the letter. He understood the members of his flock. In ancestral background he was one of them. Being a transplant himself, he appreciated the difficult adjustments the migrants had to make. He taught that the Almighty was always at your side even if you didn't always recognize His hand. When he told you that the Lord was ever-ready to help you, he followed it with the idea that the Lord helps those who help themselves. He was a preacher the men respected. According to good Lutheran tradition, they expected a long discourse - but on one occasion when his opening remarks took an hour and fifteen minutes, he skipped the sermon altogether.

JOHANNES AND JOSIE MORSTAD

The young couple who wanted a wedding and asked Tonseten to marry them. This he did at a gay celebration. Years later the minister baptized three of their children, in whom Tonseten took a special interest. He enjoyed dropping in to see how they were faring. When he did Johannes always had a special drop of welcome.

O'HARA

Another of the Irishmen whose strange name, so puzzling to Beret, was on the land marker.

OLE

(Pronounced Ola; often referred to by the diminutive "Olamand.") Per's oldest son, whose Americanized name later became Ole Haldor Holm. Ole was more of a worker than his brother Hans, who was not much younger. He was phlegmatic and determined. Like all Norwegian boys he was expected to be a scrapper. Ole was no exception. In some of Ole's tussles with his brother, Rolvaag was undoubtedly reminiscing about his own adventures on the long way home from school which afforded plenty of opportunity for unsupervised sport. Rolvaag seems to enjoy telling of these boyish fights.

PAUL

This is the name given to the child whose death caused the mother to be insane with grief. Since this name was omitted from certain editions of the novel, it has been speculated that this name was connected in some way to the fact that Rolvaag's child who died was called Paul.

PEDER VICTORIOUS

(Affectionately called Permand, comparable to our Peterkin.) This is Beret's child born on Christmas Eve. He was christened at once. On an impulse, Per gave the child his unusual middle name, a poetic variation upon Victor. The name became the title of Rolvaag's sequel to *Giants in the Earth*.

PER HANSA

If we can understand the impulse that made Per Hansa name this firstborn child of the settlement, Peder Victorious, we will have learned much about the hero's character development. The birth occurred after a long period of frustration on the part of Per Hansa. He had watched the lovely young girl he had almost stolen from her parents turn into a mixed-up disheveled woman whose interest in her family and her everyday life had nearly disappeared. He failed utterly to understand her. To a man as used to success as Per, failure in any degree is crushing. It made him weep. This big man, who could drive himself to superhuman feats of physical exertion, threw himself face downwards and cried. His failure to understand his wife was all the more heart-rending because he loved her more than life itself. He would do anything to help her. But what should he do?

He was not stupid. He was a good businessman. He was an excellent judge of other men. In certain situations, he was all mind. Where his wife was concerned, he was all heart. He is all one or all the other. In this quality of "all-ness" lies the key to his personality.

When, on Christmas eve, his mind slowly came to realize that Beret had lived and that she had given him another son, his heart leapt up. It hit the sky. He became inflated. All feelings of failure vanished. He had won. Everything had come out all right. Her achievement in bearing a son was his success. Per Hansa was victorious. The new Per was Victorious. The name is an emotional name. A new flesh and blood life becomes a symbol of all life. The new Per and the old Per are extensions of each other. At this point, in his portrayal of his hero, Rolvaag reaches the apex of his art. His viewpoint is thoroughly, personally, and uniquely his own and not an adaptation of another man's philosophy.

SIMON BAARSTAD

One of the Tronders with whom Per became friendly almost at once. It was he who extended Per the credit to buy the acre of woodland that proved to be a lifesaver when the fuel ran out.

SOFIE

Hans Olsa's daughter, who was ten years old at the beginning of the book. She is the feminine counterpart of Per Hansa's boys. In winter she is their schoolmate and in summer the chief errand-runner between the two families.

SORRINA (PROPERLY SORINE)

Sofie's mother and Hans Olsa's wife. She is the matriarch of the book. She is the one female who faces up to the prairie and wins. The men struggle with nature. She struggles with the men, their wives, and their children. She is in love with life in the same way Per Hansa is. She, too, sees life as an adventure. She lacks, however, his idealism. She is not of the all-or-nothing kind. She is practical, a compromiser who is always willing to take the bad with the good. She is the ideal helpmate for Hans Olsa who, from the materialistic viewpoint, is the most successful of the settlers.

THE SOLUM BOYS

The bachelor brothers Henry and Sam are both hard workers but are so lonesome they almost quit. They are the only two English-speaking members of the settlement. During the early first winter when they are persuaded not to leave, they become the schoolteachers - first for the children and then for the adults too. Their school, which every family wants to be at its house - even the childless Tonsetens offer theirs -specializes in storytelling and singing. As a community enterprise it becomes a great boon, even though the "teachers" let themselves in for a great deal of good-natured teasing.

STORE HANS (MEANING BIG HANS)

Ole's brother, Beret and Per's second son. He is a boy who idolizes his father. Like his father he is full of fun. Like his mother he is sensitive. As a personality he seems flawless. Everybody likes him for his kindness to his mother when her increasing strangeness puzzles them all. Once he saved an embarrassing situation when Beret had put something down where she couldn't find it. "It looks as if your eyes were in your way, Mother!"

SYVERT TONSETEN

The busybody of the settlement. Sometimes he seems more of an old woman than a man. He likes to be first - first with news, first to welcome, first to plant, first to reap, first to be consulted, first to be elected. He takes on functions that nobody else wants but which he believes bring him extra status in the settlement. He is comically unaware of his exaggerated opinion of himself. He doesn't know how afraid he is. In depression he seeks relief in an excess of gaiety, a gaiety that sometimes is so forced that it appears gross. The fact that his wife is childless is a great disappointment. He tries to compensate by being a good father to everybody. This desire sometimes turns him into a nuisance, especially when he tries to assume leadership. He has a big heart but is completely ineffectual.

TORKEL TALLAKSEN

One of the Sognings, a later group of arrivals in the settlement. He brings with him considerable more capital than the others. He has some grandiose ideas and is given to bragging. He irks Per Hansa almost from the start. In an **episode** in which he announces his intention to build a frame house he offers Per a job in such an offensive way that Per has all he can do to control his anger.

GROUP NAMES

The Hallings

Emigrants from the Norwegian district of Hallingdal. When he tries to sell them potatoes, Per feels so sorry for these poor newcomers he gives more than he sells, and even throws in a load of melons.

The Helgelanders

These folk make up the original members of the colony. Helgeland is the Norwegian district just below the Arctic Circle.

The Sognings

Emigrants from the Sogn district, made famous because of the great scenic beauty of the Sognefjord.

The Tronders

From the district of Trondhjem. Ancestral rivals of the Helgelanders who became their best friends and neighbors in their adopted land.

The Vossings

From a district not far from the Sognefjord - the Voss, a mountainous district of great natural beauty.

The Favorite Animals

Brindlesides, Kjersti's cow; Rosie, Beret's cow; Sorin and Perkel, Per's oxen; Injun, the pony, the gift from the Indians to Per.

Old Marie

The antique shotgun.

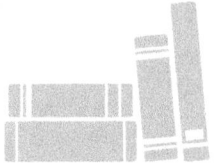

GIANTS IN THE EARTH

CONTEMPORARY SOCIETY

In 1920 when Rolvaag was devoting full time to being a professor of Norwegian literature, even going so far as to teach the Norwegian classics in English translation, another Norseman won the Nobel Prize for Literature. Knut Hamsun received the award for his novel of land-breaking called *Growth of the Soil*.

Hamsun, who had been a street-car conductor in Chicago, wrote this novel when he was sixty years old. Of all his works this is probably the least typical. It was, however, probably the only one of Hamsun's books that Rolvaag, as professor and American, would have commended and enjoyed. There are several characteristics of this book that Rolvaag emulated. This cannot be said of Hamsun's earlier successes, which were often bitter and satirical of contemporary life. The last books of Hamsun, Rolvaag never lived to see. Hamsun, who did not die until he was past eighty, went down in disgrace after publishing a weak justification for having collaborated with the Germans during the Second World War.

The prize-winning *Growth of the Soil* had unquestionable influence on *Giants in the Earth*. At fifty Hamsun had withdrawn from a varied and busy life among artists and writers. By this time he had begun to pity modern man, particularly the city-dweller. He had been called asocial, a wanderer. He deprecated American liberal-capitalist-industrial society.

Born of peasant stock in southern Norway, he went with his family to the north when he was three. At sixteen he returned again to the south and worked in a local small-town store. It is surmised that here he had some bad experience because in his books the country store is frequently depicted "as the forerunner and panderer of the lures of the city." At eighteen he was trying to write in Oslo (at that time still called Christiania), where he picked up jobs of any sort to avoid starvation. Disgusted as much with Norwegian literary life as with his economic plight, this arrogant young man came to America, where he did a stint as farmhand in South Dakota just as Rolvaag was to do not too many years later.

Ralvaag, whose ancestors were fishermen, was, as we know, no lover of farm work. He was a lonesome lad but one who bounced back from his homesickness when he began to meet townspeople, learn a little English, flirt some, and take in a newspaper. His strong Northern determination and resourcefulness added to his personal bent toward optimism and guided him into education, which was dominated by Lutheran pioneer-ministers.

The discouraged farmhand Hamsun turned to Chicago, odd jobs, and a bohemian sort of life revolving around books and lectures which would today be labeled as the "beatnik" variety. All of this resulted in a nasty little volume Hamsun called *The Intellectual Life of Modern America*. This book, regardless of its brashness, had as one of its ideas a **theme** that Hamsun was later to develop and reiterate, and one in which Rolvaag thoroughly concurred. Writers, said Hamsun, should probe into the unconscious life of man.

Back in Norway in 1890, when Rolvaag was fourteen and his family during the long winter nights were reading the tales of Bjornson, Hamsun published the first of his successful novels, *Hunger*.

Hamsun addressed himself to the intellectual elite, the only Norwegians he valued. Lofoten fishermen were not in this class. Hamsun was under the influence of the German philosopher Schopenhauer. Although Schopenhauer had been dead for thirty years, his philosophy that life is evil suited the disillusionment of the young Hamsun. *Hunger* is without a moral lesson and has no social significant. It was nevertheless sensational. It shocked.

The hero of *Hunger* has no human relationship with any other character. He blunders through life. With each mistake he indulges in a greater feeling of guilt. His inner life becomes the true subject of the novel. This Hamsun, whose purpose here was the same as the American novelist Henry James, created with great skill. In his depiction of what went on below man's surface, a tension is built up that holds the reader fascinated, if not pleased.

Like other great writers he made use of trifles to show up a man's true self. These details cause a character to betray himself. His people do more than reveal themselves. They betray themselves to no real purpose. Hamsun did not exhort his readers for their betterment. His concern was merely to depict life. Accordingly, he attacked Ibsen publicly in 1891 for his moralizing and preaching. He vehemently proclaimed that old men like Ibsen had served their time. Not social problems but individual problems deserved the attention of the young writers. This individualistic interest he exaggerated in *Hunger*, where he satirized society and particularly city life.

Regardless of these facts, *Hunger* made him a literary lion. The book was saved by its lyrical passages and by the romance that is inconsistently a part of the stark lyricism. Hamsun's understanding of female psychology was acute if not always flattering to the sex.

THE NEOROMANTIC

With *Pan*, Hamsun turned away from the squalor of the city and produced descriptions of forest and mountain. At this point we would suspect he was growing into the novelist whom Rolvaag was later to admire. However, he is still far away. These rural pictures, which were revolts from the urban scene, were far too ecstatic for Rolvaag's love of the simple. Hamsun's return to nature showed the influence of Rousseau and won him the fitting epithet of Neoromantic. There was too much sophistication in his artistry. Hamsun said, "I am trying to present something of nature worship, the sensibility, the supersensitiveness of a Rousseau - like soul."

Although its probable effect on Rolvaag was minor, *Pan* is considered important as an early contribution to the stream-of-consciousness technique. Hamsun was experimenting with word power. He used words to give unexpected effects. Rolvaag's use of sea **similes** and **metaphors** was deliberate, but the effect added a beat and rhythm to his prose that sometimes "floods" the reader and "immerses" him in the story. In *Pan* we have a deliberate exploitation of symbolism that creeps and steals into one's mind. The title *Pan*, which was chosen after the completion of the book, is a reflection of a pantheism essentially different from Rolvaag's more orthodox Christianity. Pan's ancestors are pagan.

Per Hansa in *Giants in the Earth* lives in a mud hut because he has no better. The hut is never any more than a temporary dwelling while he is extracting the fruits of the earth that are to provide riches. Glahn, the hero of *Pan*, lives in a hut so that he can be primitive, live on game and wild berries, escape society, and commune with nature. The primitivism is contrived. Glahn, antisocial and anti-intellectual that he is, requires fellow beings and also the company of women. There is no romance here, as there is in the relationship of Per Hansa and Beret. Rather, there is sex. In one instance this is even a tender affair. A young girl is attracted to Glahn and yields to him with sweetness and affection. That she had been forced to marry an old fisherman is first unknown to Glahn. Nevertheless, the situation is adulterous and as such would never have appeared in Rolvaag's writing. Even more inimical to Rolvaag would have been the fact that Glahn was not in love with the girl but was instead deeply enamored of another young lady, daughter of the richest man in the town and a complicated study in middle-class psychology. Glahn's love for her is unreasonable. He shocks a picnic party by unexpectedly throwing her slipper into the fjord. At another gathering he spits into the ear of his rival.

Rolvaag was forced to disagree with Hamsun but he could not avoid his influence. Hamsun's skill as a writer was too powerful. This he developed in a series of novels so that in later middle age, when his early scars had faded, he could turn to a **theme** similar to that of *Giants in the Earth*, and win a Nobel Prize. *Growth of the Soil* is a pioneer story that came out several years before *Giants in the Earth*. It is a story of the cultivation of virgin land and the building of a farm that takes place in the Norwegian foothills. For Americans it does not have the interest of *Giants in the Earth*, but most students of Western world literature would probably say it is a finer literary achievement. Rolvaag wrote only one big book, *Giants in the Earth*. In the same sense, Hamsun's *Growth of the Soil* is his one big book. However, Rolvaag's early books are all about emigrants and their lives in America. Rolvaag's philosophy and his **theme** are essentially the same. Soon after *Peder Victorious*, the sequel to *Giants in the Earth*, Rolvaag died. Hamsun, on the other hand, in *Growth of the Soil*, wrote a book that was completely atypical to his earlier works and afterwards returned again to his virulent attacks on contemporary society.

Even though *Growth of the Soil* was the least characteristic, it was the most read, translated, and influential of Hamsun's works. It is the story of a young man who stakes out government land for his own. He works with steadfastness. He has great physical strength and innate shrewdness. He is lonesome but is aware that he cannot expect a woman to share with him the discomforts of the wilderness. He is accordingly overjoyed when a healthy, well-shaped girl offers to live with him. Her only blemish is a congenital harelip. She is grateful to him and he to her; and soon a deep affection ensues, especially after she has borne him two sons. Nature is kind and the farm prospers, copper is discovered, and the couple are no longer poor. Other settlers begin to arrive. All of this is quite similar to the early pages of *Giants in the Earth*. Then in the Hamsun story the mother gives birth to a girl with a harelip, whom she murders within moments of her birth. From here on there is little resemblance to Rolvaag's **theme**. Later on, the woman becomes very religious. Hers is a religion, however, that is very different from Beret's. Beret imagines her sins: Hamsun's heroine commits them, and in committing them enjoys them. It is only when she feels guilty that she turns to religion. When this happens, Hamsun stresses the healing quality of nature. In Rolvaag Beret can be healed only by a God who is not only Nature but more than Nature.

STORY STRUCTURE

Giants in the Earth has two endings; one occurs at the birth and emergency christening of Peder Victorious; the second, with the destruction of Per Hansa. This split was deliberate and partly caused by the Norwegian publication of the story as two separate books appearing one after the other. This was a publisher's sales device but it does mar the unity of the book. Although the movement is swift, the scenes are episodic. They are gripping and dramatic, as are Ibsen's but the disparities of time and place are not unified. This has elicited comparison with Dickens, whose novels also were written for publication in installments. In Rolvaag the main unifying force is character growth, which is, of course, like Dickens', superb. We must remember that Dickens was read at Rolvaag by the young Ole Edvart.

If one insists that a work of art must have a beginning, a middle, and an end, *Giants in the Earth* doesn't succeed. Willa Cather in her pioneer novel, *My Antonia*, achieved this unity by means of the device of telling a story within a story. Hamsun uses the device of interjecting another character, the god from above, who wanders in and out of the story, ties one **episode** to another, and keeps the stream of consciousness always flowing in the same direction - downhill, to be sure.

THE GAME OF LOVE AND LIFE

Nothing helps like love to bring out a man's nature. As a corollary to this viewpoint Hamsun's characters make love a game by which two people can find out about each other. In Rolvaag's Per Hansa and Beret two people started out wildly, foolishly in love with each other and, because of this, their understanding or misunderstanding of each other is sympathetic. Love isn't a game to be won but a game you can be happy in losing - in other words, not a game at all.

The claim, made by the contemporary existentialist Sartre, that love is self-frustration is akin to the psychology of love that Hamsun tried to reveal in his characters. In *Pan*, where love is supposed to be a simple, natural appetite, it fails, and is frustrated because the mind interferes. It is betrayed by being observed by the lovers. In Hamsun's hero, Glahn, we have an acutely sensitive man very different from Rolvaag's Per Hansa, who is frequently insensitive. However, when Per fails in love, he knows it and because of his failure his love grows. When Glahn fails, he is unaware and love dies; however, he thinks he is dying for love. Glahn even engineers his own death. He has another man kill him. This death is very different form Per's. Beret causes the death of Per because she loves him. Her love is as intense, as foolish, and as mixed-up, as truly love, as when she first met him.

Love is a moody thing with Hamsun. Glahn is childishly peevish when he hurls the slipper into the fjord, and the girl is even sillier when she pays a boatman a big sum for retrieving it. This comedy is performed in front of the other picnickers. Hamsun's characters have all the attributes of love; Rolvaag's have more than attributes. Hamsun's avow that love will last unto death; Rolvaag's, silently, go beyond death.

THE IMPERFECT CHRISTIAN

Kierkegaard, the father of existentialism, said Christianity was an impossibility, an insanity. Bjornson, Ibsen, and Rolvaag agreed but said one had to keep on trying to be a Christian even though the ideal was unattainable. Imperfect Christianity is not absurd. Hamsun influenced Rolvaag in his attempts to equate God with nature and the universe. He agreed with Hamsun that one should live in touch with heaven and earth and the deep-rooted things of nature. He sympathized with Hamsun's search for the inner movements of man that go unobserved in remote corners. He agreed that, separated from nature, people grow rootless and corrupt. Along with Hamsun he deprecated the Christianity of the termserving, mundane ministers of the State Church. In *Giants in the Earth* the minister is the true shepherd of his flock.

Hamsun and Rolvaag both advocated that man should return towards a more elemental state. Does modern society laugh at the "troll stage" of its civilization? How much does man, in order to live, still have to take on faith? How absurd is it to have faith in the absurd, the trolls, the good and the bad they stand for? There are references to devils and eerie business in *Giants in the Earth*. Rolvaag is aware of evil, but he is firm in his conviction that man can do something about it. In this aspect he moves forward from Hamsun. Hamsun never had any intention to make life over. Rolvaag did.

In Hamsun we have suicides, fornication, illegitimacy, homosexuality, theft, all the deadly sins. Even so there is an artificiality about their deliberateness. In Rolvaag, the closest approach to evil is a mild blasphemy but this swearing has a reality about it almost never to be found in Hamsun. In choosing Isak, the self-sufficient breaker of the earth, as hero for *Growth of the Soil*, Hamsun intended to depict a simple man and his mate. He couldn't do it. Ironically, Hamsun himself, when he retreated into the country where he hoped to be himself, couldn't do it. The world interfered. War and the Nazis. He learned late, long after he had won the Nobel Prize, long after his best writing had influenced Rolvaag, who had by that time died, that man is never self-sufficient. Rolvaag never had any such illusion. Rolvaag was much more accurate in his estimates of man and life, even though he wasn't as brilliant in his manipulation of words and form.

Rolvaag was somewhat afraid of Hamsun's influence. In his lectures on Norwegian literature he wanted his students, almost all second- or third-generation emigrants, to respect Norwegian culture. He knew Hamsun was atypical. He pointed out that Hamsun had come to America because he was unsuccessful in Norway, whereas most of their forefathers had come because of a spirit of adventure, a Viking daring. Hamsun had failed in America too. Life was too much for his artistic nature anywhere. He didn't understand reality. Environment and heredity are the causes of all the man's troubles. The naturalism of Zola made life a hopeless affair. He had Isak say, "None of us can be as we ought." Rolvaag was glad that Hamsun was willing to recognize a sense of the "ought." It showed that Hamsun, regardless of his **realism**, had a sense of ethics. Nevertheless, he felt compelled to call attention to the fact that in Hamsun "You will find a thick odor of sensuality. . . . It may in particular individuals arouse passions and thereby exert an unwholesome influence."

HYMN TO YOUTH

It is ironic that while Rolvaag was lecturing to his students and worrying about the wisdom of their reading Hamsun, he was being accused of being Hamsunesque. The conservative clergy of Norway were condemning *Giants in the Earth* as being too earthy. They thought the ending where Per, leaning against a haystack in death as in life, is pictured facing west, was "horrible." They also said Rolvaag was "sexy." They even objected to the book's few mild curse words. They suspected that the **episode** of the cow and the bull as obscene. This sort of criticism is difficult for contemporary Americans to understand. It was most disheartening to Rolvaag. He had hoped that the clergy would take the leadership in his crusade for a return to tradition, culture, and religion. He had counted on the church's support. He had failed to realize how intolerant some of his fellow Lutherans had become. More and more antagonism between him and the Scandinavian fathers of Minnesota and the Dakotas became audible. To a man who felt so deeply and who had worked so long and hard for the church and church organizations, the criticism was heart-breaking.

A lesser man would have given way. Instead, Rolvaag bounced back with the spirit of youth. He lectured to the young people. He scolded them as hard as ever. He laughed at them as usual. He played the same games with them. He was one of them, more heartily than ever. He accepted engagements for speeches. He initiated a radio program. He fought for the survival of Norwegian culture and the survival of what he considered true Lutheranism with more vigor than ever before. As he worked he kept on planning more and more projects. Fortunately, with the success of *Giants in the Earth*, he had a little more economic freedom. Unfortunately, this was followed by a worsening of his health.

The publication of *Giants in the Earth* is a romance in itself. Because of its success in Norway, Rolvaag was most anxious to see it come out in English. Rolvaag had next to no contacts with the American publishing world. He had, he believed, a choice of two approaches: to submit the Norwegian version to an American publisher who might arrange for the translation, or to pay a flat fee to a translator of his own choosing and then submit the result to a publisher. Actually, Rolvaag did both. Alfred A.

Knopf of New York turned down the original with the excuse that the firm had enough other translations on its list. This discouraged Rolvaag but, nevertheless, he went ahead with a private translation. It was while this was in progress that he met Lincoln Colcord, who was first attracted to Rolvaag by reviews he had read of the Norwegian version. Colcord, who happened to be spending the winter in Minnesota, was well acquainted with the New York literary world. He called Rolvaag to the attention of Mr. Eugene F. Saxton of Harpers. A long association of the three men was accordingly started. Harper's acceptance of *Giants in the Earth* was a profitable event for all concerned. The Book-of-the-Month Club selected the book before publication. Harpers has published not only several editions, the last in 1965, of *Giants in the Earth* but also the sequel *Peder Victorious* and other Rolvaag stories.

When Colcord wrote to Saxton on March 7, 1926, he said of Rolvaag: "He retains in a rare way the viewpoint of the man with both feet on the ground - smokes a cigar to the very butt, swears fluently, and is chiefly interested in the elements of life. At the same time he has acquired much of the college professor, a certain sternness and precision of mind along with his boyishness."

GIANTS IN THE EARTH

CONCLUDING COMMENTARY

Before attempting to make a final evaluation of Rolvaag, it is necessary to take a careful look at the man and what he was doing when he came to write *Giants in the Earth*. First of all he was forty years old and had undergone many varied experiences. As a professor of Norwegian literature at St. Olaf's College in Minnesota he had traveled a long way from the fishing banks off Helgeland. He must be examined from two viewpoints: as a teacher at the height of his career and as a naturalized American citizen who had made several trips to his homeland but always returned to the home he and built on Manitou Street, Northfield.

ROLVAAG AND HIS CONTEMPORARIES

As a professor of Norwegian literature, he had more than a passing knowledge of his country's literature from the sagas onward, in all the forms of both poetry and prose. It was said in the Introduction that Rolvaag is difficult to classify as an American writer. This is also true of his place in Norwegian literature, but there is a difference in that there are some well-known names in Norwegian literature whose influence is, by comparison, easy to identify. Similarities to Henrik Ibsen, Bjornstjerne Bjornson, and Knut Hamsun are conspicuously evident throughout Rolvaag's work. These men are deep-seated influences that became internalized in an artist as sensitive as Rolvaag and in a teacher and scholar as thorough as Rolvaag. How different each of these three modern Norwegian writers was from the others none knew better than Rolvaag. He wanted to emulate them all. Recognizing the impossibility of this he copied none. Shake them off, however, he could not.

THE NATIONAL SPIRIT

His first enthusiasm was for Bjornstjerne Bjornson (1832-1910). Bjornson was forty-four when Rolvaag was born and Rolvaag was thirty-four when Bjornson died. These dates gain in importance when it is recalled that the big hall at Rolvaag was a reading room as well as a place to dry and mend fish nets. The early works, the somewhat sentimental stories with the happy endings of this long-lived author were home favorites when Rolvaag was a boy who loathed school but liked to read. The late plays which brought world renown to this same man appeared after Rolvaag had turned farmer in South Dakota and "took in" a Scandinavian newspaper. Bjornson, said H. H. Boyesen in *Essays on Scandinavian Literature* (1895), "is the first Norwegian poet who can in any sense be called national. The national genius, with its limitations as well as its virtues, has found its living embodiment in him. Whenever he opens his mouth it is as if the nation itself were speaking. If he writes a little song, hardly a year elapses before its phrases have passed into the common speech of the people ... from the drawing-room to the kitchen, the street, and thence over the wide fields and highlands.... His tales, romances, and dramas express collectively the supreme result of the nation's experience."

Instead of addressing himself to the Norwegian aristocracy and middle class, whose taste in literature and been dominated by "useful books," often **didactic** in character, Bjornson found himself writing for and about the peasantry. He considered the peasants the true Norwegians, who had not only survived long years of foreign rule but also had kept alive the historic Viking spirit of their forefathers. He inspired the people with a consciousness of their own worth which ultimately had great political effect.

Rolvaag, even if more conservative in his politics and less familiar with the local Norwegian scene, shared Bjornson's enthusiasm for revival of the Norwegian national spirit. He was dedicated to the idea that the old Norse literature was the private property of Norway and Iceland and not of Scandinavia as a whole. Rolvaag was in Oslo, Norway, in the fall of 1905. He undoubtedly was on the streets with the rest of the population to watch the pomp and ceremony that accompanied the choosing of Prince Carol of Denmark as the King of Norway. This coronation settled the issue of republic or monarchy and at the same time cut the ties with Sweden that had persisted since 1814. There is no question of Rolvaag's being just another Scandinavian. He was Norwegian!

As Bjornson returned to the common people for subject matter, so he also returned to their tradition for style. He deliberately modeled himself on the sagas. There is a grim weightiness to him that lends authority to few words. In his attempt to be brief he sometimes became obscure. Years later Rolvaag had this same tendency toward brevity in words, but one cannot say he was ever obscure - subtle perhaps, but not obscure.

Bjornson's taciturnity is rarely balanced by the humor with which Rolvaag seemed to bubble. Rolvaag had a twinkle in his eyes that kept him from being over school-teachery. Both men have a message. Bjornson carried the torch for a revival of the national spirit. Rolvaag wanted second-generation Americans to keep alive their ancestral culture as an influence to counteract a raw and unbridled tendency to materialism in their rich new country. As a standard bearer Bjornson may have been the more successful. But more on this point later.

The early novels of Bjornson are said to be weepy. Bjornson's characters cry even though their problems are those of everyman. In Rolvaag people weep only when, as in Per Hansa's agony, their problems are insoluble. Bjornson's women are motivated by love; his men, by desire for power. Rolvaag adds fear of love as part of the female character, and in the men power is compounded with love. Rolvaag's heroes and heroines are too knowledgeable, too alive, and too sensitive to each other to be truly simple.

Although Rolvaagi was not a cloistered college scholar - e.g., he took to the highways and byways to raise money for St. Olaf's; he took an active interest in the affairs and administration of the Lutheran Church; he held office in societies formed to preserve Norse culture; he on occasions addressed comparatively large gatherings - he was nevertheless not a public figure. Bjornson was. His abilities covered many fields. He was a theater director, an editor, and a public speaker for national, political, social, and educational reforms. He was of Norway and for Norway, always critical and articulate. He belonged to the great reading and listening public. Rolvaag wrote for individuals. He tried to reach inside a reader. Men liked his directness and sense of humor. He was popular with individuals, but collectively he had no great following. Students had bursts of enthusiasm for him but for the most part he was too sober for them. He always had a yearning for a public, but he feared he didn't know how to obtain it.

Naturally he was delighted when *Giants in the Earth* became a best seller, but how surprised he was, too!

To write a successful novel or play was secondary to Bjornson. He was interested in putting across his idea that national history must be the basis for national life and continued growth. Bjornson idealized Norwegian history. The old sagas were the inspiration for his plays. Like the sagas they were often tragic, but in being tragic they served as incentives for the people to shake off their inertia. He was against drinking. He favored educational opportunities, greater freedom for women, religious tolerance. In all of this he was unquestionably sincere, but because the public looked up to him so much as a person, it is no wonder that he sometimes deluded himself. Sometimes he couldn't resist the oratorical manner. As a consequence, in private life he was often accused of acting tastelessly and in literature he sometimes, toward the end of his career, committed the most obvious of flaws. (Rolvaag was to realize all this much later, when enthusiasm for Ibsen drew him away from Bjornson.)

THE GENTLE READER

Rolvaag was deeply moved by Bjornson's narratives and by the pathos in many of his situations. Rolvaag copied his sagalike directness. He admired Bjornson's skill in handling people's feelings. Often when a person is deeply moved, he can't open his mouth. How does a novelist or a playwright handle a character who is unable to talk? It takes some discernment to realize that what the character does not say is important but more discernment to understand that a character can say nothing by talking.

In his gradual progression from tales of simple parish life to novels of contemporary urban society, Bjornson becomes a master at handling conflict. The fisher lass who moves to the big city can get involved in Darwinian theory and Christian ethics. Women learn their road to greater freedom by way of discovering the beastliness in men. We have alleged lovers, divorced husbands, drunken libertines. Nevertheless, we always know whose side Bjornson is on.

As he grew older, Bjornsons' sense of the dramatic became more mellow. He is still on the attack, but his target is now generally not some moral or social abuse but a state of mind that is unrealistic or hypocritical. He grew away from stress on Christian dogma and emphasized personal morality and decency. Rolvaag would have welcomed such a change in the man. As a good Lutheran and as a teacher in a religious college, Rolvaag was orthodox in his views, but he was also tolerantly aware that true morality was not dependent upon dogma.

When the young Rolvaag emigrated, one of his first letters home contained a quotation from Bjornson: "Some day, I think, I shall reach the goal, Far, far beyond the mountains." This early enthusiasm carried through his student days. There is a report in an undergraduate paper at St. Olaf's of Rolvaag's giving a reading of Bjornson for the entertainment of his fellows. He had a great and evident admiration for Bjornson's virility and his strength in the campaign for the political and cultural renaissance of Norway during a time of internal upheaval. Rolvaag knew that political and economic unrest had been primary reasons for emigration, the justification for which he was slow to accept.

Later when he began to teach, his first classes in Norwegian literature opened with Bjornson's *Peasant Tales*. He counted on Bjornson's optimism, bounce, and great faith in life itself to jar the apathy of his students. He wanted them to remain pioneers. The ground may have been turned and sod huts replaced by frame houses, but he felt that there was still much spiritual and cultural pioneering to be done. The prairie had been conquered at a price that had drained the Viking who must rise again.

THE FIREBRAND

Just as there was an early Bjornson who wrote idyllic poetry and idealistic novels and a late Bjornson who created highly cosmopolitan dramas, so there was an early and late Henrik Ibsen. Rolvaag started early to read early Bjornson and followed the progress of the man's work sequentially. Ibsen, on the other hand, gained his popularity with the Norwegians late in his life, so that the general public had to go backward in time to acquaint themselves with his work. They read early Ibsen, such as *Brand* and *Peer Gynt*, after his later dramatic successes had appeared. It is interesting that Rolvaag did not know about Ibsen's *Brand* until he read about it as a newly arrived immigrant in South Dakota. He wrote to Chicago for a copy and was carried away by its fire. "But strange enough the fire did not make me warm and comfortable as fires ought to do. On the contrary, it chilled me through and through to the very marrow of my bones. But that chill did something for me. It made me run on and on and on. And I am not so sure but what it keeps me running still. This is sure, however, that if I in an idle moment get to think of *Brand*, I just cannot sit still."

It must also have encouraged him that *Brand*, a verse drama of Norwegian snow, icy waters, rugged mountains, and bottomless fjords, was written after its author had left his fatherland. *Brand* was written in Italy, where it gets as hot as it does in South Dakota. When Rolvaag read *Brand* Ibsen had already returned to Norway after an absence, except for one brief visit, of more than twenty-six years. During the years

1876, when Rolvaag was born, to 1896, when he first arrived in America, Ibsen had written his famous plays: *A Doll's House*, *Ghosts*, *Enemy of the People*, *The Wild Duck*, *Hedda Gabler*, and others. Of these, *Ghosts*, which now often, appears on American television, was considered too radical for European theatres. It opened in Chicago, not in English but in Norwegian, in 1882, and didn't have an English production until 1891 in London, when Ibsen was over sixty years old. Later, when Rolvaag became an authority on Ibsen, this negligence on the part of the English irked him. Like many Americans at the turn of the century, he disliked England and the English.

As a twenty-five-year-old college freshman Rolvaag wrote a book review of Ibsen's play *Emperor and Galilean*. Youthfully, he misinterpreted the play. Afterward (but before he wrote *Giants in the Earth*), when he and the rest of the world knew a great deal more about Ibsen than was known in 1901, he took pains to correct his mistake. Both the misinterpretation and the correction are interesting because their content so obviously had a bearing on Rolvaag's literary perspective. In Ibsen's play *Maximus* forecasts a "third Kingdom." Rolvaag, who as a young college student still thought of becoming a clergyman, interpreted the first kingdom as the kingdom of fallen man; the second as the kingdom of redemptive Christianity; and the third as the kingdom in existence after the Galilean (Jesus) had accomplished his purpose and man has his individuality restored. In fact, Ibsen had the Greeks in mind for the first Kingdom and a combination of the best of Christian devotion and Greek humanism for the third. It is the ideal of such a synthesis that obviously influences all of Rolvaag's mature work.

Rolvaag was a long time in reaching the opinion that Ibsen surpassed Bjornson as a Norwegian literary figure. In clinging to Bjornson Rolvaag was following the trend set by the reading public at home. Even after Ibsen's great dramatic successes Bjornson remained ahead. Bjornson's popularity started early. It was his failure to be awarded the "poet's pension" that had already been granted Bjornson that made Ibsen leave for Italy, "in disgust.."

In Rolvaag's capitulation to Ibsen, late as it was in coming, he ran counter to Norwegian opinion, which said in effect that Ibsen embellishes and enhances the body of Norwegian literature but is not typical of it. Many Norwegians take the same attitude toward Rolvaag. If this position seems curious it is also understandable. Ibsen and Rolvaag were in their art decided individualists. Individualism is a Norwegian characteristic often said to be caused by the country's geography, in that so many of its people lived in small communities isolated by deep fjords and ice-bound mountains. Because they were left so much alone, these people prided themselves on their resourcefulness and ability to solve problems in their own way. For generations they were hostile to conformity and then came Bjornson, an advocate of nationality at a time following political chaos and long years of outside domination. With Bjornson also came a scientific awakening and an opening of communication lines which revolutionized many traditional ways of living. The stress on individuality was eclipsed, and the comforts of conformity came in. Neither Ibsen nor Rolvaag is a comfortable writer.

Ibsen's *Brand* has already been referred to as chilly. Brand, the leading character, is a Kierkegaardian figure. He is uncompromising and unbending. His **theme** is "all or nothing." He is a firebrand of a young, itinerant minister who sacrifices his child and then his wife and at the end himself. This hero was followed two years later by another extreme **protagonist** faced in the opposite direction, Peer Gynt. Peer (Kierkegaard from a different perspective), is unprincipled, irresponsible, absurdly buoyant and yielding. Both figures are **epic** in character, both are reminiscent of the heroes of the sagas but at the same time are out of step with the Norwegian temper of the time. As would be expected, Ibsen conceived them as heroic and chose verse for his form, which again didn't contribute to their popularity.

As a result of this unpopularity many Norwegians, and certainly most Europeans, first learned of Ibsen through his later "problem" dramas, which were translated almost at once into German and French. In this dramatic form, if not in content and spirit, Ibsen was following Bjornson, who used his plays for reform purposes. Both men were following the literary movements of realism and naturalism that were moving across the Continent.

Rolvaag, as a teacher of language, studied these trends. He knew too that they moved back and forth on the American literary horizons via their various European exponents. Rolvaag disliked both "**realism**" and "naturalism" intensely. He thought they belonged in the gutter. He was, in 1910, still the idealist who contended that literature, though affected by the times, should influence the times. It took ten years of life and its disappointments to disillusion him.

By 1920 Rolvaag had grown to admire Ibsen and some others whom he called realists for their detailed knowledge of human psychology. The mature Rolvaag found his fellow beings very complicated. At the same time, he was afraid that Ibsen in his **realism** was losing the idealism he had displayed in the early *Brand*. Rolvaag felt that art had to be idealistic, that it had a requirement to rise above ordinary existence and show mankind a vision of a better life. The realities of life, upon which Rolvaag brooded with intensity after the death of his son, Paul, had to be transcended. There had to be a synthesis of **realism** and idealism.

Such insistence was part of Rolvaag's fighting spirit. Part of this fire within him was kept burning by *Brand*. Ibsen had accentuated Rolvaag's tendency towards single-minded pursuit of a goal. Rolvaag had as his chief aim the maintenance of Old World culture in raw America. He would not give up. He believed in his message with the "all-or-nothing" force of *Brand*. Rolvaag saw himself as he once had dreamed of being, a fighting young minister.

STRUGGLING IDEALIST

No one knew better than Rolvaag how hard it is to remain an idealist. In his struggles he, like every other human, was his own worst enemy. When he turned all his thinking powers upon the **realism** of the mature Ibsen, he practically had to deny what he saw in order to hold to his ideals.

In Ibsen's play *The Wild Duck* we have, among other themes, a brutal attack on self-deception. By remaining an idealist, Rolvaag certainly knew he was guilty of certain dishonesties, but he justified these because he was in love with life and he couldn't live either as an artist or as a man without ideals.

Rolvaag knew Ibsen too well, the man's blunders as well as his achievements, to imitate him. For one thing he didn't believe that the theatre was the place to teach a lesson. Rolvaag didn't write plays. He was of the conviction that theatregoers wanted to be entertained. He questioned Ibsen's right to make them think in their seats. Only an Ibsen could provoke the people into listening to discussions, to problems, and even to accusations through five acts. The stage is constructed for actors. A play is make believe. It is not meant for **realism**. Rolvaag stuck to his novels, which could be read in silence and solitude.

Rolvaag studied Ibsen's complicated characters. He was fascinated by Europe's new absorption in matters psychological. He recognized the influence of Freud upon all intellectual affairs. An individualist himself, he fathomed the depths of Ibsen's characters who came to life as individuals. Rolvaag's characters are just as lifelike as Ibsen's, but vastly different nonetheless. Very few of Ibsen's characters are likeable. Very, very few of Rolvaag's are unlikeable.

Ibsen had moved from the stormy Norseman in *Brand* and the goatish Cinderella in *Peer Gynt* to characters who represented the pillars of society; these were often enemies of the people. Norwegians were often skeptical of these problem people. They failed to see any "poetic vision" in Ibsen's analyses. Rolvaag insisted that both *Brand* and *Peer Gynt* were such an internal, if not integrated, part of Ibsen and of all Norwegians, himself included, that one couldn't put on an Ibsen play without these two characters turning up somewhere. Rolvaag felt that the trouble rested with the Norwegian critics, who were unable to generalize about Ibsen. He defied classification.

LOVE AND DESIRE

Rolvaag learned from Ibsen, but first of all he learned from life. Nowhere in Ibsen is there a couple like Per Hansa and Beret. Nowhere in Ibsen is there a love story. In Ibsen there is desire, or respect, or pity, or understanding, but not love. It is almost possible to divide Ibsen's heroines into those who shunned love and regretted it and those who yielded and regretted. His people are dedicated or disciplined on the same basis as *Brand*'s all-or-nothing. They seem to seek answers to their problems everywhere but in themselves. They are unfulfilled. Rolvaag's Beret has aspects in her character that remind the reader of Ibsen's heroines. When she first comes out into the prairie and sees the wide, unbroken vistas, she exclaims, "There's no place to hide." In this she is like Mrs. Alving in *Ghosts*, who tries to hide from life. But unlike Mrs. Alving, whose husband and lover were scoundrels, Beret had her one and only Per. He was her Brand and Peer Gynt rolled into one, her fulfillment.

HUMOR

Ibsen had still another quality that, fortunately, was missing in Rolvaag. Ibsen was almost completely without a sense of humor. Rolvaag could be as serious and as uncompromisingly realistic as Ibsen, but as his hardworking students knew, there was suppressed laughter behind that straight face. The reader of *Giants in the Earth* who sometimes feels himself exhausted by the tension and tragedy of an **episode** is relieved - quickly, suddenly - by the entrance of a character like Tonseten. Tonseten, who embodies laughter, keeps Rolvaag from falling into Ibsen's quagmire of overseriousness. The American critic H. L. Mencken thought this was an artistic inadequacy on Ibsen's part, whereas others thought his ability to sustain the serious was a dramatic triumph. Ibsen forced attention by asking profound questions of his audience. He didn't answer them. Rolvaag, as has been said, did not provide answers either, but he treated his readers "gently" by pointing out and thus eliminating what was not an answer.

SYMBOLS

Rolvaag did not follow Ibsen's treatment of the symbolic. Rolvaag's **similes** and **metaphors** of the sea, of the house, of the kingdom, of the web are scattered throughout the pages of *Giants in the Earth*. This process puts seed in the ground from which, hopefully, it will bear fruit. Ibsen is not so trusting. The wild duck is one of Ibsen's most famous symbols, and he puts it into the title, *The Wild Duck*. To this same play he adds a dog. The reader must figure out what these symbols mean. In Rolvaag the trolls symbolize the beasts in men, but we don't have a chapter headed "The Troll." One explanation offered for Ibsen's contrived symbolism is that Zola, the so-called father of naturalism, was his mentor.

The American writer who appeared not too long before Rolvaag was Frank Norris, whose *McTeague* was admittedly a naturalistic novel of California in the Zola manner. In this story gold, in all its forms from gold teeth to gold bird cages, symbolizes greed. Such was not Rolvaag's manner.

Ibsen and Rolvaag are both indebted to the Danish Kierkegaard, the progenitor of existentialism. Both were searchers for the truth. Both left their homelands. Ibsen left Norway because he was poor and unrecognized. Rolvaag left primarily out of a spirit of adventure as a modern Viking. He was the one to settle in a new land, but remained ever proud of the land he left behind.

FREUDIAN PSYCHOLOGY

Ibsen's characters are marked by their protracted self-analyses. Rolvaag's characters are too busy earning a living. Environment and heredity are subjected to scrutiny (Zola fashion) by Ibsen. Environment and its effect on inherited characteristics had been so thoroughly pondered by Rolvaag in his understanding of people that he takes them for granted. This he can afford to do because the people in his books have the same environment and the same cultural backgrounds. He doesn't place a character of one background alongside another of different background for the sake of drama. His people are individual because they love and because they are kind to each other. They want to help each other. They learn about each other from observation of each other's daily lives. A person is as he is today. You explain him today as you watch and love. You make up your mind about him from the immediate and not by an analysis of his ancestors.

Rolvaag was a student of psychology. His was a psychology not of sickness but of health. It is true that in *Giants in the Earth* Beret is sick to the point of insanity. There is, however, always some health in her, and she makes a recovery. Rolvaag was too much of a realist to make the recovery complete, but she does recover enough to be a loving and useful person. Ibsen's characters are sick and evil.

This does not mean that Ibsen was on the side of evil. It is usually agreed, especially today and outside of Norway, that he was psychologically and morally right. When one looks at his plays as a whole and makes a list of the dramatis personae, one cannot discount his fascination with evil. Ibsen says people know they ought to be good but are bad anyway. Rolvaag says people are mostly good and when they are bad, let us not make matters worse by talking about it.

Rolvaag, who was a man of strong urges, who found support in religion and work, could, it is suspected, describe evil with accuracy. In Ibsen, play after play contains a problem grounded in some sexual **episode**. Not so in Rolvaag. In *Giants in the Earth* Per Hansa, a healthy giant of a man, certainly had a sexual problem when his wife's mind failed. We read that for him to have touched her in her childlike condition would have seemed incestuous to him. Rolvaag takes pains to inform the reader that Per was in difficulties. He wants us to know that this is psychological motivation for some of Per's behavior. Rolvaag does not tell the reader what to think. He allows the reader to speculate. Did this man go outside of his home for sexual gratification? Would he have been justified? Did he spend himself in work? Was he overconcerned for his children, his reputation, his worldly success? Rolvaag doesn't say. One thing, however, that he does say (and it is a thing Ibsen never could say), is that Per never stopped loving Beret. Ibsen would have analyzed such a love as an obligation or as the claim of an ideal, or as an attack of morals.

Ibsen was a riddle to Rolvaag. In one of his lectures quoted in the biography by Jorgenson and Solum, Rolvaag, said, "Ibsen is constantly insisting that the duty of one's life is to realize one's self. How that realization will be possible he does not make clear to us. For the free exercise of will in the dramas results in disaster. Are we therefore to conclude that one must make compromises? . . . I think not. Life is tragic. Hence the idealist who attempts to reform society will be crucified. But if there were only enough idealists who would let themselves be crucified, the world would soon be better. That, I think, is also Ibsen's view."

In Ibsen's early work *Brand* the her loves his worldly fight, but the reader is led to believe that because of his loss he gained his soul. This is not a new concept. It is basic to much religious thought. It has been reiterated so often that its value has been dissipated. Rolvaag was often disturbed by the glibness to which preachers and teachers are so often prone. Since he had started out by teaching the Old Testament and was frequently a lay preacher, Rolvaag often caught himself being self-righteous. It is easy enough to recognize this in others, but one can be blind about oneself. This was a propensity he had to struggle against. After the death of his boy, Rolvaag became increasingly tolerant of weakness in others but less tolerant of himself. To be a man you had always to be in control of yourself. You had always to fight. An inner battle is ennobling. If one went down, it was all the more necessary to come up fighting. Ibsen had this same idea and Rolvaag admired this in Ibsen more than Ibsen's art, his artistry, his knowledge of psychology, and his understanding of "naturalism" and "realism." Rolvaag adopted whole-heartedly the opening lines from Ibsen's *Cataline*. He repeated it with frequency to his students: "I must, I must, a voice in me is calling. Deep from my soul, and I will follow it."

Easier said than done! Rolvaag insisted that Ibsen, though he wrote realistically, was a "pessimistic idealist." He could have been commenting on himself. After he had been teaching a long time, even after he had consented to extend himself by offering Ibsen courses in English and after the success first in Norwegian and then in English of *Giants in the Earth*, Rolvaag became pessimistic about his ideal. Had he been right in his campaign to keep Norse culture alive in America? Would the sons and daughters of the pioneers follow in his footsteps? Would they be enriched? Did they need such an anchorage? Had Ole Edvart Rolvaag failed?

Admit such a possibility after a lifetime of effort? Rolvaag would not do it. He turned to Ibsen's *Wild Duck*. There is more than one lesson in this play. For example, there is in the play a very practical-minded doctor who experiments and who is an enthusiastic devotee of the new psychology. He believes that for health's sake many people need a certain amount of fantasy or self-delusion. They must deceive themselves or die. Rolvaag said to himself that unless he kept on believing that he was right in his life's work, he would die. Rolvaag chose to live. Another lesson that Rolvaag took from the play concerns the Wild Duck itself. A wild duck should remain a wild duck. If the duck is wounded, if it has a broken wing, it should not be tamed. It should be allowed to die.

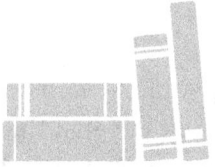

ESSAY QUESTIONS AND ANSWERS

Question: The heroism of Rolvaag's pioneers consists in battles with nature. Describe two such battles.

Answer: There are two outstanding battles with nature. The most dramatic is Per's single-handed struggle to survive in a blizzard. The most disheartening is the onslaught of the grasshoppers.

Almost at the very beginning of the snowstorm, which started more like a sucking whirlwind, Per and his ox team were separated from the other wagons. The ropes that the men had used to lash the caravan together snapped when both the animals and their drivers were blinded by the waves of snow. Per's eyebrows became ledges of frost through which he tried to squint. The oxen plowed into a drift but Per wouldn't let them come to a halt. He feared they would freeze to death and he with them. With almost superhuman strength he rubbed them, beat them, drove them on as he stumbled on foot alongside. Regardless of his concern for the beasts and his life, anxiety for his wife was uppermost. For her sake he kept going and won the battle.

Not so successful was the struggle the pioneers waged with the grasshoppers. At a moment when all the settlers were rejoicing because they were bringing in their first crop of wheat, there arose what they first thought was another dust cloud. Instead, thick gusts of hopping, screeching insects swarmed upon them. Every blade of grass, every hair on man or beast was covered. The scourge was so frightening it made Beret take her two youngest, crawl into the big chest, and close the lid. They lost this battle with nature, as they did year after year when the pests returned.

Question: Discuss the basic symbolism in *Giants in the Earth*. Is it easy to recognize?

Answer: The movement of the pioneers from civilization to their mud huts is repeatedly symbolized as a sea voyage. The settlers move from the shores of civilization onto the sea of the prairie. In the opening pages of the novel when Per Hansa's dilapidated caravan is lost in the glare, the last wagon, with Rosie, the cow, tied on as it were like a rudder, moves through the tall grass. The beaten-down stalks make a wake which soon is lost in the waving mass.

On the last pages of the book, when Per is setting out in the whirling snowstorm so that he may get a minister for his dying friend, he takes his bearings from outlines of the settlement and lays the course he thinks he should follow. He goes forward, even on skis, in steady strokes as though he were rowing. Then almost like a sailor his thoughts turn to the home he has left and before long he loses his course. But no matter, the wind holds steady . . . to the end.

The symbolism of the sea is rarely absent more than a few pages at a time. Rolvaag's early life on ocean waters as a fisherman and as a fisherman's son was so deep within him that the **metaphors** and **similes** often literally crest on each other.

Question: Discuss the role of the Hansa boys in *Giants in the Earth*.

Answer: When their parents are struggling with nature and the effects of nature on their taut nerves, the trusting faith of childhood comes to the reader's attention with welcome relief. The two older boys, who can play and fight and make up, are typically boyish even though they differ one from the other. Both are comforts to their parents. Ole, the older, is a responsible youngster who copies his father and tries to do a mansized day's work. He can even cuss a little when things go wrong. Store Hans knows when his mother is upset. He can change her mood when he thinks it's necessary - sometimes with a joke. On the other hand, when he doesn't succeed, he can run out into the woods to hide his tears.

The boys serve to break the tension of the adult story. They appear on the scene at the right moments. When the settlers are on edge at the arrival Indians and are trying in vain to eat a normal supper and when Per decides he has to investigate the Indian camp, Store Hans jumps up and goes with his father. On the way Per begins to talk of scalping. Store Han's questions spare the reader's nerves. After the Indians have peeled off a scalp, Store wants to know, does it grow in again? What do the Indians do with a scalp? The father's mind is elsewhere. Maybe they make mittens out of it. "You're only fooling," cries Store Hans.

Question: Per Hansa destroys the land markers of the Irish settlers. Does Rolvaag approve of this action?

Answer: There is little doubt that Rolvaag approves of this action regardless of the fact that this may not be the viewpoint of orthodox religion. The deed also runs counter to the old

Norwegian tradition. To destroy the property stakes of another is worse than thieving among Norwegian peasants, who have no better way to protect themselves than through the forces of unwritten and moral law. It is because of this age-old attitude that Beret is shocked when she sees him chop up and burn the stakes. In destroying the evidence of his deed he shows how much he too is aware of the fact that his act may be considered a crime.

Nevertheless Per does what he does deliberately. He has weighed both sides of the situation and decides it is better for the settlers, among whom he is a leader, not to be driven out by the Irish, whose claim to the land he thinks is a fraud. He is the boss who takes responsibility for what he considers the long-run good. He feels he has to act immediately, even before the treachery of the Irish is proven.

What Rolvaag considers wrong is not the act but the fact that Per, having been proved right, boasts about his deed. There is no doubt that his boastfulness is partly due to psychological relief. He has been anxious and suddenly his guilty feelings are gone. Even so, Rolvaag has Hans Olsa rebuke Per by saying that Per had been rash and that, had not the Good Lord been on his side, he would not have been successful.

Question: How does Per Hansa resemble earlier heroes in Norwegian literature? How does he differ?

Answer: Per Hansa has been compared to Brand in Ibsen's early poetic drama of the same name and also to Isak in Hamsun's late novel. *Growth of the Soil*, which won the Nobel Prize. The "all-or-nothing" philosophy of Brand is strongly evident in Per Hansa's determination to succeed in the land of his adoption. He refuses to be subdued by nature. He refuses to recognize his wife's need to return to civilization. He gives his all when most men, including the other pioneers, would relent. Even his love for Beret is on an "all-or-nothing" basis and here, paradoxically, is his undoing because in his love he fails to understand her love. He differs from Brand in motivation. Brand is motivated by God from above, and Per is motivated by man, from within.

Hamsun's Isak is also a first settler on new land who also drives himself. He, too, is independent and strong. He despises men who are weak. He wants no truck with town life. He loves his farm and the family he raises there. Unlike Per, he doesn't battle nature. He is at one with nature. He acts naturally. When his wife, according to her own nature, offends society, he doesn't condemn her. Neither does Hamsun. Rolvaag stands between the rigorous, messianic religion of the early Ibsen and the loose pantheism of Hamsun.

Question: Compare *Giants in the Earth* with Willa Cather's popular story of pioneer life, *My Antonia*.

Answer: Miss Cather's book has enjoyed wider acclaim than Rolvaag's. There are several reasons for this, although one may dispute their validity. In the first place Miss Cather wrote in her native English. *Giants in the Earth* is the author's and Lincoln Colcord's version of the original Norwegian. Accordingly, Miss Cather's prose is more consistent and her organization more unified. On the other hand, her writing has been criticized as being overstylized, too smooth, especially when compared to the rough vibrance of Rolvaag. In the same sense, her device of telling a story within a story appears to many to be artificial.

This device is typical of the "stream-of-consciousness" technique that was gaining popularity with the more experimental English and American novelists of the time. The episodic quality of Rolvaag's stories is out of step with this trend. Both Miss Cather and Rolvaag have been labeled romantic realists. They are certainly both realists in the sense that they both write with exactitude and that their characters are very lifelike. It is in the "romantic" part of the phrase that they differ. Miss Cather's romanticism lies in her attitude toward love. Some find her too sentimental in the depiction of a little bit of bad in every good girl. Rolvaag is romantic in his situations. They are unusual, perhaps sometimes wildly strong, but never picturesque.

When she wrote *My Antonia* Miss Cather had already achieved success with earlier novels. She knew her public and she knew what the publishing and literary worlds expected from her pen. Like a journalist she had fluid mastery in her writing. She had a confidence in the rightness of her art. Rolvaag had the same attitude to his art but more than that, he had a purpose in writing. He had a message - that new America desperately needed Old World culture. This conviction adds a natural strength to his writing that Miss Cather had been forced to learn through practice.

Question: Beret has been called a "mixed-up personality". How do heredity and environment cause complications?

Answer: The naturalism of the French novelist Zola, of which Frank Norris in *McTeague* was the earliest American exponent, was based on the concept that man is the product of heredity and environment. Rolvaag was a man of his times and as such went along with the much-discussed Darwinian theory concerning the evolution of man. He saw no conflict between it and religion. Even some Lutherans were shocked by his attitude. Beret had inherited the religion of her forebears. She knew the comforts of European civilization. She knew a home where the heirlooms of centuries added a security of well-being. She knew her parents wanted her and her husband to stay in Norway, where they were assured of economic security, if not glittering wealth. The Bible told her to honor her father and mother. Her husband was determined to leave. Here arose the conflict. In the New World, the hardships, the cruelty, and the crudities of life confirmed her conviction that she had done wrong. Then as she watched her husband's joy at material success, she was sure he, too, had done wrong. She began to imagine other sins. The conflict within her, because she never stopped loving him, grew deeper and deeper. She had no one to talk to, least of all her husband. She invented people to talk to. Finally, she holds conversations with her mother, who she believes dead. She even prepares a meal for her. She is pitifully deranged. Paradoxically, she regains her sanity through the efforts, good sense, and prayers of an itinerant minister, whose Christianity is of the old, old world, older than Norwegian medievalism.

Question: What significant contribution does the minor character Tonseten make to the novel as a whole?

Answer: Tonseten is an example of Rolvaag's sense of humor and his tolerance of the weaknesses in human beings. Rolvaag was a humble person. He always knew that the world had better teachers, better scholars, better writers, better artists than he was. There were also better and healthier men who made better friends and better husbands and fathers. We can't all be brilliant. Rolvaag was sympathetic and patient with fools. Tonseten is such a fool. Rolvaag treats him kindly, as does Kjersti, his wife. Pompous and unaware of his pomposity, Tonseten is lovable. One pictures him with his thumbs in his suspenders, with his red beard bobbing up and down, as he pours out words of wisdom with ever-increasing speed and ever more obvious ribaldry. He must be listened to, this important little man.

Sometimes when he can't convince himself that he is the great man he wants to be, he goes on short visits in the hope that for the sake of hospitality a drop of liquid cheer will be offered him. It usually is. The settlers are, as a rule, glad to have him about, He is hard-working and generous, even if a little muddled. He is matter-of-fact and outspoken on the elemental affairs of life. He fancies himself a Romeo - how harmless no one knows better than his wife. He is less popular with the men, who sometimes pity him and sometimes take advantage of his good nature. He is so weak and inconsistent that he acts as an excellent foil to his indomitable neighbors, whose strength is sometimes overwhelming.

Question: Per Hansa risks his life to get a minister for the dying Hans Olsa. Why does Olsa mean so much to Per?

Answer: Olsa is the lucky troll. He is an Askeladd from Norwegian folk literature. Through him Rolvaag, and in turn, Per Hansa, stands aglow remembering the dreams and yearnings, the secret strength and determination of the fairy-tale heroes who reflect the aspirations of the Norwegian people. Olsa was Per Hansa's inspiration. This barge of a man is the reason why Per joins the caravan. He continues to be, even after the settlement had weathered its first storms, their steersman. Like Askeladd, whose genius was first hidden, Olsa is the awakened man who becomes the good emigrant. He is the most successful. He has the best luck with his cattle. He develops the finest herd. He builds the finest house. These achievements are the result of his inventiveness and resourcefulness against all odds. He enjoys doing things. With the drive of the starry-eyed optimist, he is an unassuming natural leader of men. He has seemingly inexhaustible physical courage. This is the man Per Hansa emulates. Can Per believe, when Olsa sickens from overexposure in a storm, that he is afraid to die? Per's wife tries to convince

Per of this. She fails. Nevertheless, Per recognizes Olsa's desire for a minister. If Olsa wants a minister, Per will risk his life to get one regardless of Olsa's reasons, expressed or otherwise. Olsa is facing death while the storm rages without. Per gets his skis and goes for Askeladd's sake. The Norwegian motif of the story makes this ending a necessity, realistically and psychologically.

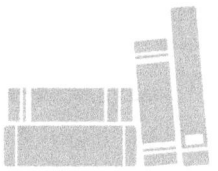

BIBLIOGRAPHY AND GUIDE TO FURTHER RESEARCH

RECENT EDITIONS OF GIANTS IN THE EARTH

1965 Perennial Library, New York, Harper & Row. This paperback includes the author's original foreword to the English edition and also the original introduction by Lincoln Colcord, who was the cotranslator with the author from the original Norwegian.

1964 Harper Torchbook, New York, Harper & Row. This includes the author's foreword but omits the introduction by Lincoln Colcord. A new introduction by Einar Haugen of the University of Wisconsin was substituted. Paperback.

1929 Harper's Modern Classics, New York, Harper and Brothers. This contained an introduction by the editor, Vernon L. Parrington. This introduction was reprinted as "Ole Rolvaag's *Giants in the Earth*" in *Main Currents in American Thought* (New York, 1930), III, 387-396.

1928 New York, Harper and Brothers. This edition closely follows the original.

1927 New York, Harper and Brothers. This is the date of the first edition in English and contains the introduction by Lincoln Colcord which appears in the 1965 paperback.

1929 A tragedy from the novel also called *Giants in the Earth* was written by Thomas Job and was also published by Harper and Brothers.

OTHER ROLVAAG NOVELS

Peder Victorious, translated with Nora O. Solum, New York, Harper and Brothers, 1929.

Their Father's God, translated by T. M. Ager, New York, Harper and Brothers, 1931. (These last two books are sequels to *Giants in the Earth*.)

The Boat of Longing (original 1921), translated by Nora O. Solum, New York, Harper and Brothers, 1933.

Pure Gold (original 1920), translated with S. Erdahl, New York, Harper and Brothers, 1930.

OTHER NORWEGIAN WORKS AVAILABLE IN TRANSLATION THAT INVITE COMPARISON

Bjornson, Bjornstjerne, *Happy Boy*, in Harvard Classics, New York, P. F. Collier & Son. First published in Norwegian in 1860.

Bojer, Johan, *The Emigrants*, translated by A. G. Jayne, New York, Grosset & Dunlap, by arrangement with The Century Company, 1925.

Hamsun, Knut, *Pan*, translated by W. W. Worster, with an introduction by Edwin Bjorkman, New York, Alfred A. Knopf, 1921.

Hamsun, Knut, *Growth of the Soil*, translated by W. W. Worster, New York, Alfred A. Knopf, 1921, reprinted 1953.

Ibsen, Henrik, *Ghosts, The Wild Duck, An Enemy of the People*, with an introduction by Benfield Pressey, New York, Rinehart & Co., 1948.

Ibsen, Henrik, *Brand*, a new stage version by James Forsyth, with an introduction by Tyrone Guthrie, New York, Theatre Arts Books, 1960.

Ibsen, Henrik, *Peer Gynt*, translated by William and Charles Archer, with an introduction by William Archer, New York, Charles Scribner's Sons, 1908.

Undset, Sigrid, *Kristin Lavransdatter*, translated by Charles Archer and J. S. Scott, New York, Alfred A. Knopf, 1923, 1925, 1927.

BIBLIOGRAPHICAL SUGGESTIONS AND STUDY GUIDE

(The following readings are all in English)

Beyer, Herald, *A History of Norwegian Literature*, New York, New York University Press, for the American-Scandinavian Foundation, 1956. This volume includes an excellent bibliography.

Boynton, Percy H., "O. E. Rolvaag and the Conquest of the Pioneer," *English Journal*, XVIII (September, 1929), 535-542.

Colcord, Lincoln, "Rolvaag the Fisherman Shook His Fist at Fate," *The American Magazine*, CV (March, 1928) 36-37.

Commager, Henry, "The Literature of the Pioneer West," *Minnesota History*, VIII (December, 1927), 319-328.

Harper, Ralph, *Existentialism, A Theory of Man*, Cambridge, Mass., Harvard University Press, 1958.

Jorgenson, Theodore, and Nora O. Solum, *Ole Edvart Rolvaag: A Biography*, New York, Harper and Brothers, 1939. This is the definitive biography.

Kazin, Alfred, *On Native Grounds: A Study of American Prose Literature from 1890 to the Present,* New York, Harcourt, Brace & Co., 1942. Paperback.

McFarlane, J. W., *Ibsen and the Temper of Norwegian Literature*, New York, Oxford University Press, 1960.

Rolvaag, O. E., "Christian Doctrine in Ibsen's *Peer Gynt*," *Religion in Life*, I (1932), 70-89.

____"Vikings of the Middle West," *The American Magazine*, CVIII (October, 1929), 44-47.

____"The Writer's Conclusions," *Scholastic Magazine*, XIX (November 28, 1931), 6-21.

Taber, Clarence W., *Breaking Sod on the Prairie*, New York, World Book Co., 1924.

WPA Writers Project, *South Dakota: A Guide to the State*, New York, Hastings House, 1938.

New York Times: Obituary Review of Rolvaag, November 6, 1931.

EXPLORE THE ENTIRE LIBRARY OF BRIGHT NOTES STUDY GUIDES

From Shakespeare to Sinclair Lewis and from Plato to Pearl S. Buck, The Bright Notes Study Guide library spans hundreds of volumes, providing clear and comprehensive insights into the world's greatest literature. Discover more, faster with the Bright Notes Study Guide to the classics you're reading today.

See the entire library of available Bright Notes guides at **BrightNotes.com**

Available in print and digital wherever books are sold

IP INFLUENCE PUBLISHERS

www.ingramcontent.com/pod-product-compliance
Lightning Source LLC
LaVergne TN
LVHW011720060526
838200LV00051B/2967